A Pottery by the Lagan

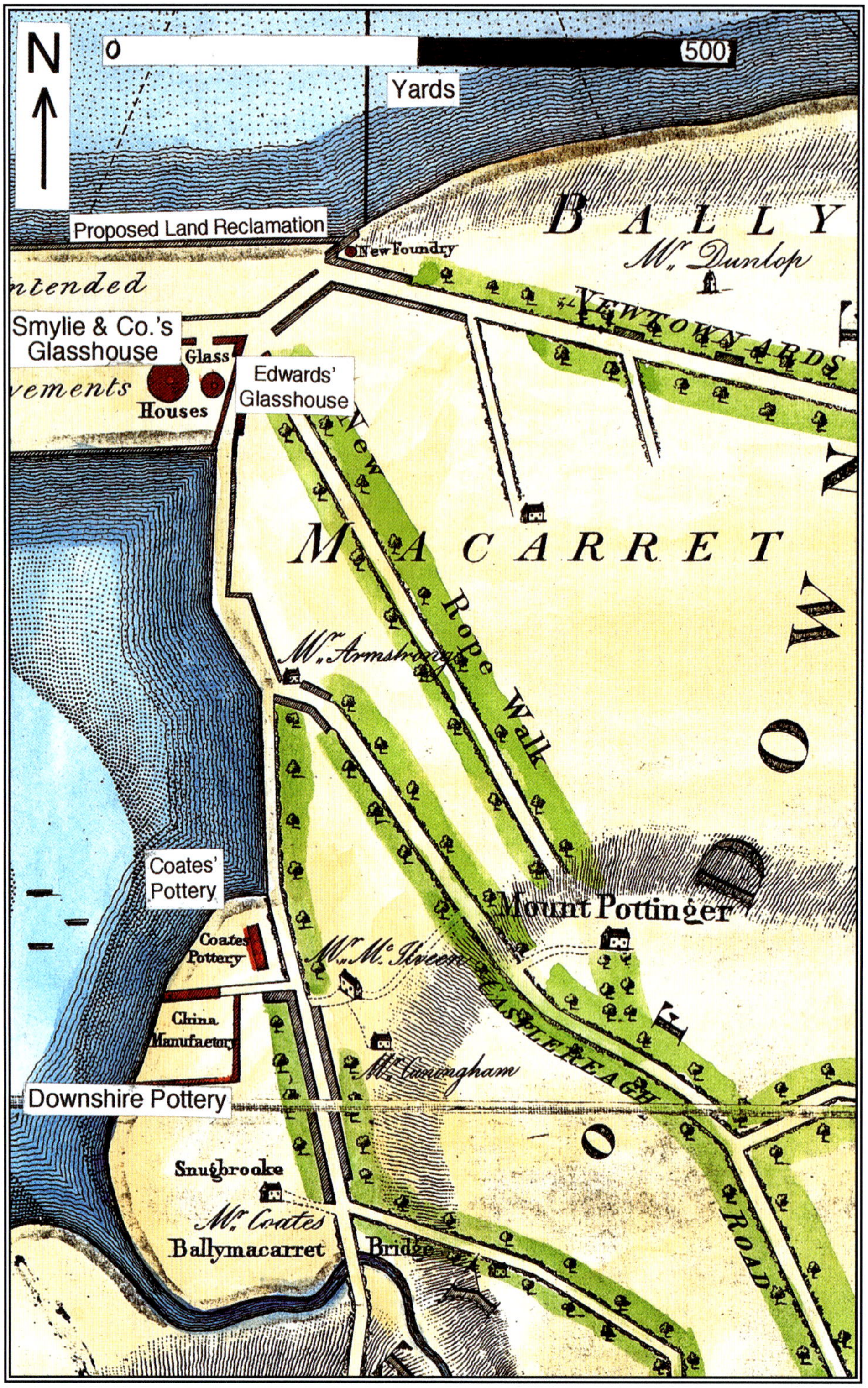

Figure 1. James Williamson's (1791) map of Ballymacarret, showing the earliest commercial development of east Belfast. With the exception of the rope works, all of the industries established here in the late 18th century were involved in pottery and glass manufacture. The Downshire Pottery and Smylie's Glasshouse were both initiated by Thomas Greg, as described on pp 6–7. (His second glasshouse, set up in 1792, is not shown.) Black-glazed earthenwares were made nearby at Victor Coates' Pottery, while Benjamin Edwards' glasshouse produced fine-quality Irish table glass several years before Waterford. Edwards' new iron and brass foundry was initially set up nearby to provide tools and moulds for the glasshouse, but later developed into a significant industry in its own right.

A Pottery by the Lagan

Irish Creamware from The Downshire China Manufactory, Belfast, 1787–c.1806

Peter Francis

The Institute of Irish Studies
Queen's University Belfast

in association with

National Museums and Galleries of
Northern Ireland, Ulster Museum

First published in 2001
The Institute of Irish Studies
Queen's University Belfast
8 Fitzwilliam Street
Belfast
BT9 6AW

in association with

National Museums and Galleries of Northern Ireland, Ulster Museum
Botanic Gardens
Belfast
BT9 5AB

British Library Cataloguing-In-Publication Data.
A catalogue record for this book is available from the British Library.

Cover:
Front: A selection of creamware vessels attributed to the Downshire Pottery, c.1790–96. See colour plates 14–16 and 20–23

Back: See colour plate 17

This book has been supported by CERAMIKA-STIFTUNG BASEL

ISBN 0 85389 694 1

Printed by W. & G. Baird Ltd, Antrim.

CONTENTS

ACKNOWLEDGEMENTS

THE research described in this book began in 1991, and now, in drawing the work to a close, it is daunting to realise that almost ten years have elapsed. Even more daunting, when finally tallied, is the number of individuals who have contributed to the project along the way. It is a pleasure to record these individuals and gratefully acknowledge the help they have given.

Dr TE MacNeill of the Archaeology Department at Queen's University Belfast was especially encouraging during the early years, first by sharing in some of the initial discoveries, later by supervising and examining my Master's thesis in post-mediaeval archaeology. Soon afterwards, the Downshire Pottery site was located, and although the present-day owners of the site have asked not to be identified, the discoveries made there would have been impossible without their generous and wholehearted co-operation, for which I am especially grateful.

Investigation of the site was conducted in two parts. The first, 'rescue' excavation was carried out with the impromptu assistance of a small group of unpaid volunteers: Emily Bennett, Raymond Bennett, Jane Castles, Valerie Cooper, Mandy Crawford, Charles ('Bobby') Dickinson, Mavis Dickinson, Rosemary Henry, Peter Meanley, Janey Sproule and Roberta Rea. A further member of this team was Felicity Graham, who provided additional, invaluable help by allowing the store-rooms of Temple Auctions to be turned into a temporary archaeological 'laboratory', for washing and sorting the finds.

The second, 'formal' excavation of the Downshire Pottery site was made possible by funding from the Environment & Heritage Service of the Department of the Environment (NI), as a result of the interest shown by Dr Chris Lynn and Nick Brannon in particular. The success of this excavation was entirely due to the enthusiasm of the team involved: Tom McErlean, Andy Dickson, Laura Francis, Melanie Reid, Vaughn Gibson and Nick Lewis. The author would like to express particular gratitude to Tom McErlean, whose involvement in the project lasted far longer than the two weeks of the excavation, and who contributed greatly to the site investigations conducted at that time.

In many respects, the excavation was only the beginning of the work. The latter stage of the research, which became known as the 'Belfast Potteries Project', was made possible by three individuals: George Mackey and Kyle Alexander of Laganside Corporation, and Professor Brian Walker, Director of the Institute of Irish Studies, Queen's University Belfast. Thanks to their efforts, and with funding provided by the Laganside Corporation, the Environment & Heritage Service, Belfast Natural Historical & Philosophical Society, the Esme Mitchell Trust and the Baring Foundation, the Belfast Potteries Project was conducted over a two-year period at the Institute of Irish Studies.

The Ulster Museum became involved soon afterwards, thanks to the initial interest shown by Dr Bill Maguire. Since then, the research has consistently relied heavily on the support provided by various members of the museum's staff, including Kim Mawhinney and Elizabeth McCrum of the Applied Art department and illustrator Deirdre Crone. The author's greatest debt of gratitude is owed, however, to Trevor Parkhill, Keeper of History, whose enduring support for the work has been truly exceptional.

Several individuals have also given assistance in providing illustrations, and among these I would particularly like to thank David Barker, Jonathan Horne, James Lennon and Mrs M Forsythe. The help that Danny Kinahan, of Christie's (NI), has given this project at various times has also been greatly appreciated.

The continuing support of the Institute of Irish Studies and the Ulster Museum has been instrumental in bringing this work to publication. During these final stages, the contributions of Margaret McNulty and Catherine McColgan of the Institute of Irish Studies have been crucial. The fact that this publication now resembles a coherent book is entirely a result of their efforts.

There are some whose contributions have been less specific in nature but vital nonetheless. Professor Mike Baillie of Queen's University Belfast has been interested in this research from the very beginning. His informed advice has always been welcome, and has made the work all the more enjoyable. More recently, Nicholas and Susan Mosse have helped greatly by providing the author with a quiet sanctuary in which to write some of the more complex sections of text. Their experience as practical, modern potters has also provided many new insights into the workings of the Downshire Pottery, but by far their greatest contribution has been the boost to morale that their obvious interest in the work has brought.

There are two people, however, without whom the work could never have been completed. The first is Linda Canning, my colleague in the Belfast Potteries Project and probably one of the most cheerful, enthusiastic individuals I shall ever work with. The project could easily have foundered if Linda had not been committed and conscientious to the very end, and the fact that the assemblage was washed, sorted and catalogued is wholly the result of her exceptional efforts. Finally, I owe my greatest debt of gratitude to my partner, Rosie Agar, who has shown great patience and given support at every step along the way, from finding the very first of the creamware shards, to correcting the final proofs of the text.

Peter Francis

FOREWORD

As Director of the Institute of Irish Studies at Queen's University Belfast, and Chief Executive of the National Museums and Galleries of Northern Ireland, we are pleased to introduce this publication on Belfast creamware. It represents the extensive research of the author, Peter Francis, which has greatly revised our understanding of the manufacture and design of Irish creamware in Belfast at an important time in its development in the last decades of the eighteenth and the early years of the nineteenth century.

Other recent published research by Peter Francis has turned on its head much of the received knowledge about Irish glass. This expertise in the fields of glass and ceramics has been enhanced by his training as an archaeologist and through historical research skills. These are very much in evidence in this innovative publication.

Before this research on the potteries of pre-1800 Belfast began, little was known of their wares. The evidence presented here will contribute significantly to a more informed understanding of the manufacture and design of creamware in Ireland, particularly Belfast, in the late eighteenth and early nineteenth century.

It is particularly appropriate that the outcome of research by Peter Francis and Linda Canning, as represented in this volume, should be published jointly by the Institute and the Ulster Museum. Peter held a Research Fellowship at the Institute for two years. The History Department of the Ulster Museum provided the funding for a one-year Junior Fellowship (1995–96) for Linda Canning as Research Assistant on the essential work of reconstituting material which had been excavated in Belfast city centre. This has now been deposited in the Ulster Museum.

The present publication not only serves as a catalogue of that material but also demonstrates for the first time the unexpectedly extensive early development of Belfast's creamware industry. It is also a timely instance of fruitful and purposeful co-operation at the level of research and publication between museum and university in a subject where their areas of expertise have been shown to be mutually supportive. We are pleased to acknowledge the contribution of Dr WA Maguire, then Head of Human History Division in the Ulster Museum, to the establishment of the Junior Research Fellowship which greatly assisted the conservation of this intriguing collection.

Any research project involving the excavation of ceramics can only be enhanced by the active involvement of experts in the fields of archaeology and ceramics. The museum is well served in each of these disciplines and the project benefited from exemplary co-operation between a number of departments. In this regard the History Department is especially grateful to the Keeper of Archaeology and Ethnography and the Curator of Ceramics and Glass in the Department of Applied Art for their informed contributions, and to the illustrator in the Department of Archaeology and the museum's photographers for their technical assistance.

Grateful acknowledgement must also be made to a number of sources of funding. The Baring Foundation, the Belfast Natural History and Philosophical Society, the Laganside Corporation and the Esme Mitchell Trust supported Peter Francis's research in the Institute of Irish Studies. Danny Kinahan, Christie's agent in Northern Ireland provided valuable support at an early stage of preparation for publication and the Ceramika-Stiftung Foundation in Switzerland provided the means to ensure that this work was published in an illustrated format which does justice to the overall significance of the research and the subject of creamware in Belfast in the late eighteenth century.

Michael Houlihan
Chief Executive, Museums and Galleries of Northern Ireland

Brian M Walker
Director, Institute of Irish Studies, Queen's University Belfast

AUTHOR'S PREFACE

For most of the inhabitants of Belfast, the fact that fine-quality pottery was once made here will hopefully come as something of a surprise. When many of us think of Belfast's industrial history we tend to think of shipbuilding, linen-making and the ropeworks, but nothing so delicate as fine-china. The reality is, however, that during the 18th century there were actually three, high-quality potteries in the city – the earliest of which preceded even the renowned shipyards and linen mills.

During the period known as Grattan's Parliament, (c.1782–1800), when Free Trade allowed Irish merchants to trade worldwide as readily as their English counterparts, considerable efforts were made to establish Belfast as a major centre of fine-pottery and glass production. Sadly however, many of the liberal reforms that were promised by Grattan's Parliament ultimately failed to materialise, so that many of these commercial opportunities, which initially seemed so promising, gradually slipped away. Under the ensuing regime, which came in with the Act of Union in 1801, industries that did not conflict with English commercial interests – such as shipbuilding, linen production and ropeworks – prospered and were remembered. Others – like pottery and glass manufacture – were gradually extinguished and forgotten, more by the strength of their English competitors than by adverse legislation.

In many ways, therefore, the story that unfolds here of Thomas Greg's remarkable Downshire Pottery (1787–96) precisely mirrors the rise and decline of Belfast's commercial spirits in the late 18th century – from the advent of the reforms of 1779–82, to the dashed optimism and spoiled investments that preceded the 1798 rebellion. The pottery does appear to have revived for a few years after 1800 – resuscitated by an imprisoned United Irishman, no less – but evidence suggests that this was a much smaller, less ambitious venture than Thomas Greg's original. Regardless of just how the pottery fared before 1800 and after, however, the fact that Downshire's wares were principally made of Irish materials means that they represent a unique experiment in ceramic history, not to mention a rare and precious memento of their times.

Considering the extent of the interest expressed locally for history and historical events, the sad fact that central Belfast has lost almost all of its 18th century buildings in the last 30 years defies explanation. The most significant finding of the present work, by far, is that two of the Downshire Pottery's buildings have somehow managed to survive two centuries of continual industrial use, and they are still in use to this day. Now that their existence is recognised, we can only hope that something can be done to preserve them. The pottery was unique in Ireland, not just in Belfast. As the only purpose-built, 'Staffordshire-type' pottery ever built here, there can be few 18th-century buildings of comparable historic importance left anywhere in the North.

The principal aim of this book, however, is modest – it is simply intended as a guide for those who might like to try to find a piece of Downshire pottery for themselves. Since the excavations took place in 1993, all of the intact pieces that appear in this book have been found, and the quest still continues. If any reader should in future discover that he or she is fortunate enough to own a piece of Belfast creamware, the author cannot conceive of a time when he would not be glad to hear of it.

Peter Francis
Belfast, December 2000

Documentary History

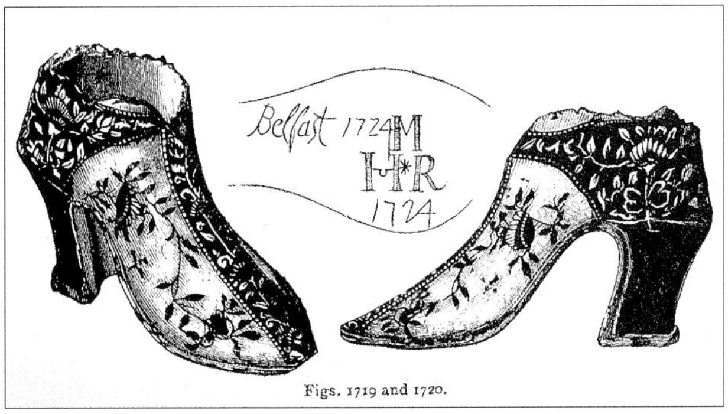

Figure 2. The Belfast Delftware 'choppine', or miniature ladies' shoe, first illustrated by George Benn in 1877 (*History of Belfast*, p 355).

Introduction

THE work described in this book began as a casual interest for the author, sparked off in 1983 by an illustration in Benn's *History of Belfast* (1877), which showed a curious blue and white pottery shoe bearing the inscription 'Belfast 1724' (Figure 2). The date seems unusually early, as Belfast in 1724 was a town of only 4000 or 5000 people, yet the ceramic of which the shoe was made – delftware – was more sophisticated than anything being produced by potters elsewhere in Ireland at the same time, even in Dublin. Could this intriguing object really have been made here, and if so, might other pieces exist?

In attempting to answer these questions, the hobby developed into a more full-time occupation. By 1992, sufficient documentary information had been gathered for a Master's thesis in archaeology, but still, not even one new and intact piece of early Belfast pottery had turned up.[1] In 1993, however, when the Downshire Pottery excavations described in this book took place, the character of the research changed dramatically, because for the first time there was ample evidence to show that fine-quality pottery had indeed been made in Belfast more than two centuries ago.

With the help and support of various individuals, particularly Professor Brian Walker at Queen's University Belfast and Kyle Alexander of the Laganside Group, funds were found for a two-year study that later became known as the 'Belfast Potteries Project', conducted at the Institute of Irish Studies, Queen's University Belfast.[2] In 1995, the Ulster Museum's acquisition of the excavated Downshire Pottery 'collection' allowed a second archaeologist, Linda Canning, to be brought in to impose order upon the jumbled mass of broken, unwashed pottery that had been excavated. The fact that this catalogue of the collection now exists is in itself an eloquent testimony to the many hours that Linda worked. As a result of her efforts, the Downshire Pottery assemblage – fully cleaned, sorted and catalogued – was formally presented in 1997 to the Ulster Museum, where it now resides.

The working dates of the Downshire Pottery were 1787–c.1806, a date range more than half a century *later* than the 'Belfast shoe' of 1724 which had originally prompted this study. The Downshire Pottery also made 'creamware', rather than 'delftware'. To explain these terms, and to understand the discrepancy in dates, we must first look briefly at the almost forgotten history of fine-ceramic manufacture in Belfast, before moving on to the Downshire Pottery itself.

We now know that there were, in fact, *three* fine-ceramic potteries in Belfast during the 18th century, which operated at intervals between 1697 and c. 1806. The earliest of these, and probably the most important in academic terms, was the 'Belfast Potthouse', which made delftware in Hill Street (just off Waring Street) in central Belfast from 1697 until about 1725. It was here that the 'Belfast shoe' was made.[3]

The term 'delftware' describes a specific type of early pottery that is still made today at Delft in the Netherlands, also known as 'tin-glazed earthenware'. Before c.1750, when delftware was at its most popular, most European potters were unfamiliar with the techniques involved in manufacturing the translucent *porcelains* that came only from China and Japan, but they were able to replicate some of their finer qualities deceptively. By applying a very thick, opaque white glaze (coloured white by tin oxide) and by using a more porous pottery 'body' than normal, they produced delftware – which gave the *impression* of being clean, white and 'China-like', but at very much lower cost. By the late 17th century, delftware had become the most popular household pottery in England, but it was not until the very end of the century, 1697, that delftware potters first came to Ireland, and to Belfast in particular.

Of all the places in Ireland they could have chosen, why Belfast? Dublin, for example, had a population of around 62,000 in 1700, compared to the 4,000 or so that lived in Belfast. The reason seems to be that the Belfast Potthouse was probably established by a local man, Matthew Garner, first recorded in London in the early 1680s when he commenced an apprenticeship as a delftware potter. After various trials and tribulations, Garner was eventually forced home to Belfast by bankruptcy in 1697, to find that several important local merchants, such as David Smith (the mayor) and Robert Leathes (the Donegall family's agent), were keen to invest in his highly specialised skills. As a small piece of kiln furniture found on the Belfast Potthouse site shows (Figure 3), the business was up and running within just two years.

The key to the success of the Potthouse was not

Figure 3. A 'trivet' from the Belfast 'Potthouse' site dated 1699. This is presently the only known example of Irish pottery bearing a 17th-century date.

Garner's potting skill, however, nor was it the money that the merchants invested. Instead, it rested on the fact that deposits of the special chalk-rich clays that were essential for making delftware were discovered just a short distance away, at Carrickfergus, on the shores of Belfast Lough. Thanks to Carrickfergus clay, the Belfast potters were to remain the only delftware manufacturers in Ireland for the next quarter-century, until about the time of Matthew Garner's death in 1725. After that, delftware manufacture was largely confined to the largest marketplace in Ireland – Dublin – where the renowned 'World's End Pottery' was established in 1735 or so by the Belfast merchant John Chambers, (who may have worked at the Potthouse originally).

Delftware manufacture did not cease entirely in Belfast in 1725, however. At some time between 1743 and 1754, a second delftware pottery was set up in Belfast in Little Patrick Street, across the road from Sinclair Seaman's Church on Corporation Street. We know very little about this venture at present, other than its location, which is shown precisely on a 1754 document. A few pieces of mis-fired delftware were recovered near the site in 1992, which do at least confirm that delftware was made there, but it is also possible that experiments were made with other, more sophisticated wares as well. Perhaps the most important feature of this pottery is that it was probably owned in 1763 by Thomas Greg, who went on to set up the much more ambitious Downshire Pottery that followed in 1787 (see p 6 for additional details). It would be much easier to understand Greg's involvement in the Downshire Pottery if we knew what kinds of wares he was making at Little Patrick Street, but unfortunately, no excavations have yet been carried out.

We have no record of the Little Patrick Street pottery after 1763, but developments outside Ireland would shortly afterwards change the ceramic industry forever. The first indication of what was to come began in 1766, when exports of Carrickfergus clay declined steeply. By 1778, these exports had stopped completely, as the manufacture of delftware ceased almost everywhere in the British Isles. The reason is that a number of innovative English potters, particularly those at the heart of the industry in Staffordshire, had developed a new type of ceramic ware, known as 'creamware'. Unlike delftware, which used a thick, white *glaze* to make the wares appear white, the creamware potters took exceptional pains to produce a pottery *body* that fired to a pure-white colour, which required only a thin, *transparent*, yellow or cream-tinted lead glaze. In use, creamware proved to be superior to delftware in every way; it was lighter, thinner, more heat resistant, and much more difficult to crack and chip. By the 1780s, when the Downshire Pottery was set up, and thanks primarily to Josiah Wedgwood's masterful marketing techniques, creamware was fast becoming the most popular household pottery throughout the British Isles and beyond. Naturally, Wedgwood's success attracted many imitators, but any Irish potter wishing to attempt the same feat faced a number of severe difficulties. Not the least of these was finding the raw materials that were necessary for making this new, superior ware in Ireland. (Carrickfergus clay, which had been ideal for making delftware, was not suited to making creamware.)

This was the task that the Belfast potters set themselves when they established the Downshire Pottery in 1787. Against this backdrop, we can now look at the story of Irish creamware more closely, to gain a clearer impression of the exceptional achievement that the Downshire Pottery represents.

THE ORIGINS OF IRISH CREAMWARE

During the last century, several authors have published accounts of Irish ceramics, focusing especially on early Dublin delftware, the largest and best understood group of all.[4] Only one study, by Mairead Dunlevy of the National Museum of Ireland, attempted to consider the much more obscure origins of Irish creamware.[5]

From this research, we now know that the Dublin Society, which offered financial rewards or 'premiums' at this time to encourage Ireland's industries, first offered Irish potters a premium for creamware manufacture in 1769. Edward Stacey, James Roche and partners, the owners of the World's End pottery in Dublin, attempted to claim this premium for the manufacture of an 'Earthenware in Imitation of… Flint or Paris Ware', but they failed to submit a ware 'of the Sort for… which the Premium was offered'.[6] Clearly, the pottery was still producing delftware at this stage (1769), even though this was now perceived as old-fashioned. Even so, the delftware that they made was judged 'sufficiently good of its kind' to be encouraged with a special award of £50.[7] They made no further progress with developing an Irish creamware, however, as the Dublin Society premium that was offered for creamware in the following year (1770) remained unclaimed.

In December 1771, it seems that Edward Stacey, the principal owner of the Dublin pottery, went into partnership with two creamware potters who had just recently arrived from England, Edward Ackers and Thomas Shelly.[8] Together, these three partners then converted the World's End pottery from a delftware to a creamware pottery in the period between December 1771 and March 1772, when creamware manufacture commenced. In addition to making two successful applications to the Dublin Society, which were quite specific in demanding an 'Earthenware in Imitation of Staffordshire Ware, or that which is commonly called Yellow-Stone Ware',[9] Stacey & Co's manufacture of creamware is confirmed by a Dublin newspaper advertisement of June 1773. In this they stated that their former delftware pottery had become a 'Paris or Queen's Ware manufactory… [which] made and sold all sorts of said ware, both useful and ornamental… gilt and plain, made entirely of the Materials of this Country… equally serviceable, and of as elegant Workmanship, as any imported, and at Prices much more reasonable than the English'.[10]

Unfortunately, for potential collectors of Dublin creamware as much as for Stacey & Co themselves, their significant technical achievement did not bring commercial success. Despite excellent initial sales, Stacey & Co experienced financial problems after just two years (from November 1773) and they failed to meet the modest third-year production target that was set by the Dublin Society from April 1774.[11] Furthermore, at least one of the two English partners, Thomas Shelly, appears to have returned to England in 1774 to set up a creamware pottery at Longport, North Staffordshire.[12] At first sight, therefore, documentary evidence indicates that this earliest of Irish creamware manufactories survived for only two to three years (December 1771–c. April 1774).

Despite the fact that no further Dublin Society applications were submitted, it seems unlikely that creamware manufacture at this Dublin pottery was quite so brief. As Dunlevy remarks, it is difficult to tell from the scant evidence available whether this pottery later 'lay idle for much of the time but was revived on occasions, or whether the pottery continued in use with occasional injections of capital and enthusiasm'. By whichever means, indirect evidence shows that some form of pottery manufacture continued.

Dublin maps, for example, continued to indicate the pottery site as a 'China Manufactory' for a further 15 years, despite revisions in 1778 and 1787, while a Dublin newspaper in 1791 discussed an attempt by some Staffordshire potters in about 1777 to make 'Queen's Ware in imitation of that of Chinese'.[13] The unreliable author John Angel may well have been optimistic in his suggestion that there were 'many' manufacturers of Queen's-ware in Dublin in 1781, but the same criticism is less readily levelled at the redoubtable Josiah Wedgwood, who testified before a House of Lords committee of a fresh attempt by some Staffordshire potters to set up a creamware pottery in Dublin in 1784.[14] Wedgwood's testimony is substantiated by the discovery that the World's End 'pott house' was sub-let in December 1783 to a Thomas Coleman by one Edward Chetham (who, like Thomas Shelly, may have been a Longport potter).[15] In June 1784, Chetham sold the pottery together with 'all that the several Earthen Goods' that it contained; an event which probably marks the true date at which attempts to manufacture creamware in Dublin ceased.

As Dunlevy concludes: 'By 1785 it would seem that Ireland had "no considerable works except the coarse kind", [while] two years later the *Dublin Chronicle* could wonder why "no adventures of spirit have availed themselves… and launched into the pottery and earthenware business in this kingdom".[16]

The *Dublin Chronicle* was obviously unaware that four months earlier, in May 1787, some 'adventures of spirit' had done exactly this on a grand scale, albeit in Belfast rather than in Dublin. The question then arises of how this major new pottery could have hoped to succeed in a small town like Belfast, now with a population of c.15,000, when the biggest and oldest pottery in Ireland had only recently failed amidst Dublin's 170,000 residents?[17] The answer lies partly in the characters and aspirations of the merchants involved, and partly in their responses to the dramatic political events that took place in Ireland during the late 1770s and early 1780s.

JOSIAH WEDGWOOD AND THE COMMERCIAL BACKGROUND

Ireland was unable to develop a sizeable fine-ceramic industry in the late 18th century for many reasons, but one individual certainly had a more profound influence upon this situation than any other – 'the greatest creamware potter of them all' – Josiah Wedgwood.[18] Even considered solely as a merchant, acting purely on his own behalf, Wedgwood represented formidable competition for the Irish potters (Figure 4). The swift demise of Stacey & Co's Dublin creamware pottery in 1771–74, for example, was probably due largely to the direct competition that it faced from Wedgwood's major retail outlet in Dublin, established just as Stacey & Co were setting up.[19] Wedgwood was to close these highly successful Dublin premises in 1777 (thereafter selling through agents), but his position as England's foremost potter and spokesman for the industry in Staffordshire later enabled him to influence much more than the fortunes of just one Irish pottery.

During the late 1770s, the demands of Irish merchants for commercial and constitutional parity with England grew to the extent that an unprecedented series of reforms was introduced by Westminster from 1778 onwards. The first and most important commercial reform to take effect (in 1778–80) was the granting of free trade, whereby Irish merchants were enabled to market their wares in British, colonial and other overseas markets. The introduction of this measure alone was sufficient for the Irish glass industry to more than double in size between 1779 and 1782 (from four glasshouses to nine), even though some significant commercial grievances remained unresolved.[20] At first, these grievances were shelved while Irish demands instead focused upon constitutional reform, but following the establishment of legislative independence in the form of 'Grattan's Parliament' in 1782, commercial matters once again resumed priority. Wedgwood was to assume a prominent role in the debates that followed.

The 'commercial resolutions' that Westminster proposed in 1785 (sometimes known as 'Pitt's Reforms') were vigorously criticised by English and Irish merchants alike; considered by the former to be too liberal, and nowhere near liberal enough by the latter. In England, Wedgwood was 'in the vanguard of the manufacturers' opposition to the propositions', so that once manufacturing interests throughout Britain perceived the need for an organisation to articulate their grievances, it was Wedgwood himself who transformed the idea into actuality by founding the General Chamber of Manufacturers (which existed solely to protest against Pitt's Irish Reforms).[21] Following the presentation to the House of Commons of 'A Petition of the Manufacturers of Earthen Ware in Staffordshire' against the measures in April 1785, Wedgwood gave testimony on behalf of all 50 petitioners to a House of Lords Committee which sat two months later.[22]

Wedgwood's 1785 testimony vividly conveys his reasons for contesting these proposed reforms, even though Ireland, at that time, did not possess a single fine-ceramic pottery. (The Downshire Pottery was not to commence until 1787.) Principally he believed that cheap Irish labour and lower duties would ultimately allow Irish ceramics to 'flood' the British and overseas markets 'at 40 or 50 per cent cheaper, on a most moderate calculation, than we can afford to sell it in Staffordshire'. He supported this patently over-stated notion by arguing that Ireland's geographic proximity to England also increased the likelihood of an exodus of skilled labour and specialist knowledge from Staffordshire.[23] A valuable piece of information which Wedgwood clarifies is that the pipe clay necessary for making creamware could not be exported from England. (It was used apparently in making gunpowder.)[24] Whatever its justification, this prohibition meant that any intending Irish creamware potter had first to discover clays in Ireland that were of similar quality to those which the English potters obtained from Cornwall, which even today is not easy.[25] Quite apart from any commercial considerations, this legislation alone probably contributed very significantly to the small size of the Irish fine-ceramic industry in the late 18th century; compared to the Irish glass industry, for example, which employed no prohibited exports in its manufacture, and hence thrived.

Wedgwood's excessive objections to the establishment of a pottery in Ireland were singled out for condemnation by the Irish press, perceived in some quarters as a 'spontaneous ebullition of intense commercial selfishness'.[26] At precisely the same time, however, Thomas Greg – soon to establish the Downshire Pottery in Belfast – was also appearing in the Irish press, acting just as vigorously to prevent the passing of Pitt's commercial resolutions as Wedgwood

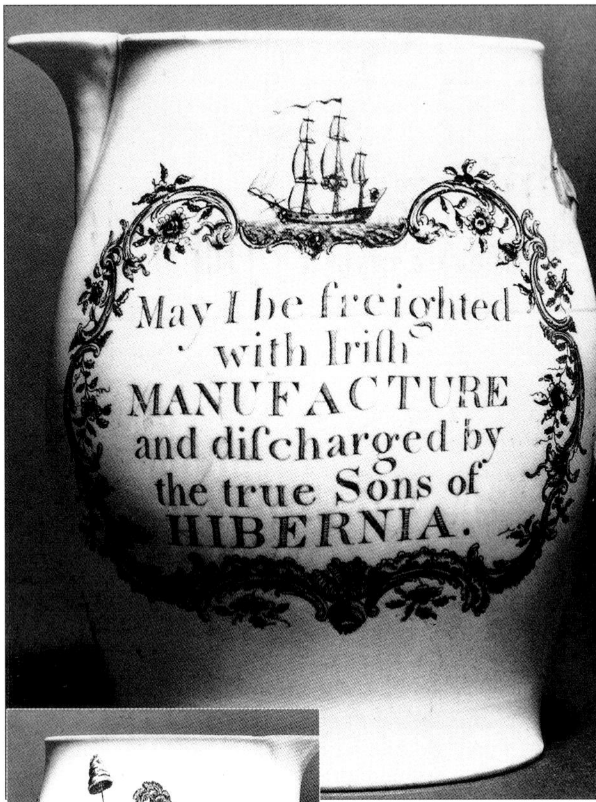

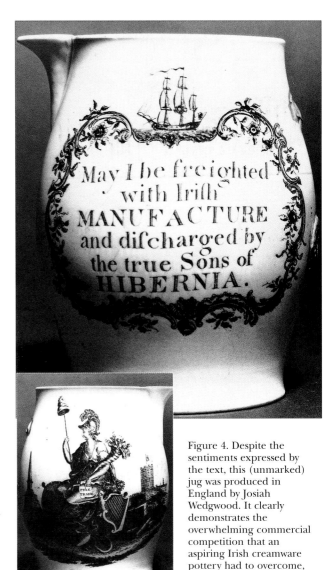

Figure 4. Despite the sentiments expressed by the text, this (unmarked) jug was produced in England by Josiah Wedgwood. It clearly demonstrates the overwhelming commercial competition that an aspiring Irish creamware pottery had to overcome, even to become established in its home market.

himself.[27] Curiously, these two merchants had arrived at this same point by travelling in totally opposite directions. Whereas Wedgwood may have hoped that putting an end to the resolutions would end attempts by Westminster to grant liberal commercial reforms to Ireland, the Irish merchant community of which Greg was a part instead viewed the resolutions as a renewed barrage of protectionist legislation. Thus, when Pitt's bill was withdrawn from the Irish Parliament in August 1785, (withdrawn rather than defeated), the expectation remained in Ireland for some years afterwards that commercial reform would still come.[28] It was in this expectation that plans for the only purpose-built 'Staffordshire-type' pottery in Ireland were undertaken, but considering Wedgwood's strongly antagonistic attitude towards such a venture, this attempt to reproduce 'a similar fabric to that of

Wedgwood' in Belfast just two years later was a highly audacious move. Perhaps a younger, more timid man than Thomas Greg would not have tried.[29]

THE FOUNDERS OF THE DOWNSHIRE POTTERY, THOMAS GREG & PARTNERS

Documentation relating to the Downshire Pottery identifies its founders as three distinguished Belfast gentlemen: Thomas Greg, Dr Samuel Stephenson and John Ashmore. Their reasons for embarking upon such an ambitious venture can best be appreciated by looking briefly at these individuals in their local context.

Stephenson was a much-respected philanthropist, a wealthy Presbyterian country minister who retrained in middle-life as a physician and settled in Belfast just two years before the pottery was set up.[30] The more anonymous merchant John Ashmore, 'a man of considerable literary culture', came from one of Belfast's old established families, and his extensive business premises were situated just a few doors from Stephenson's surgery.[31] Undoubtedly, however, the prime mover behind the Downshire Pottery was Thomas Greg (Figure 5), probably the wealthiest Belfast merchant of his day and certainly the most enterprising. Greg was 69 years of age in 1787, when plans for the Downshire Pottery were first advertised, which gives some indication of the vitality and flair of this truly remarkable man. (Ironically, the more enduring legacies of his second son, Samuel Greg, who founded the Quarry Bank Mill at Styal in Lancashire in 1783, and of his direct descendant Thomas Tylston Greg, whose famous 'Greg Collection' of English pottery resides in Manchester City Art Gallery, mean that the Greg family name now holds much more significance in England than in Belfast.)[32]

Thomas Greg's business interests prior to the Downshire Pottery were exceptionally widespread. He was the principal landlord of Lord Donegall's Belfast estates, a major property developer in his own right, a linen and cotton magnate, a pioneering chemical manufacturer, the owner of extensive lands in Russia, England and the American colonies, owner of a fleet of merchant ships (with a highly profitable 'sideline' in transporting emigrants) and a key founder-member of the local chamber of commerce.[33] He 'spent much money in searching for coal and other deposits of mineral wealth in the north of Ireland', supporting these explorations with major investments in canal-building.[34] Greg also lent his skills to various charitable schemes, and it was likely to have been for these works that he was reportedly offered a baronetcy in 1783.[35] All things considered, with the possible exception of his brother-in-law and business partner Waddell Cunningham, Thomas Greg was foremost among the 'old-guard' of Belfast's dynamic merchant community in the late 18th century.[36]

Despite his obvious commercial talents, it was difficult to understand initially why Greg should have invested so late in life in the specialised and high-risk business of

Figure 5. Thomas Greg c.1765, while still a young man. (He was 69 years of age when he established the Downshire Pottery.)

creamware manufacture, the more so in view of the scale of the pottery which he is now known to have built. Part of the answer may lie in Greg's unusual choice of business partners. Although neither Stephenson nor Ashmore had experience of a major commercial venture, Greg and Stephenson, at least, were deeply involved in the Belfast Charitable Society, set up in 1752 to cater for the poor of Belfast. (Stephenson was the Society's physician from 1786.)[37] One of its aims was to find suitable employment for the 'maintenance of Foundling and other Children', to which end a highly successful cotton mill had been established nearby in 1779.[38] Considering that Greg, Stephenson and Ashmore's later petition to the Irish Parliament makes particular mention of the fact that the Downshire Pottery offered work for 'many workmen and children', one of the attractions of setting up a pottery may have been that it offered comparatively humane employment to a large number of these poorhouse residents.[39] (The Dublin potter, Henry Delamain also advertised in 1754 that he took 'Charter school, parish or distressed tradesmen's children' as apprentices.)[40]

In addition, evidence shows that Greg had previously owned an unrecorded *delftware* pottery in Belfast during the mid 18th century. A small assemblage of wasters recovered near the site of this Little Patrick Street pottery in 1992 confirms that delftware was probably the main product, though some fragments of a coarse, lead-glazed, red-bodied ware were also found.[41] Only one piece of delftware has so far been tentatively attributed

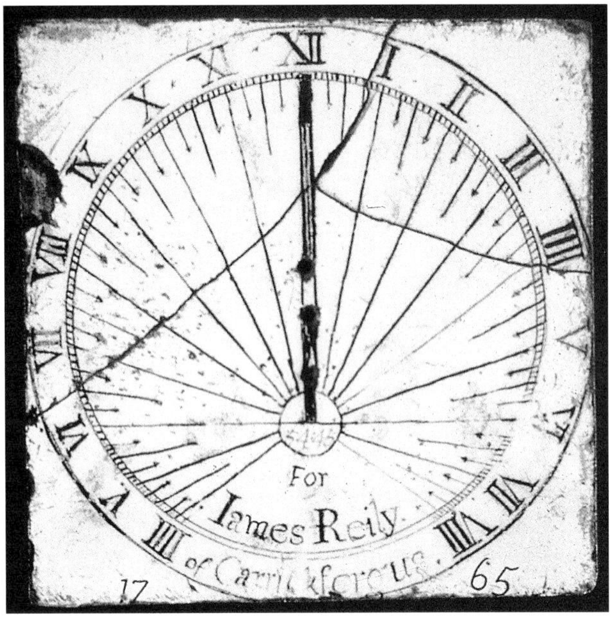

Figure 6. This modest, manganese-painted delftware sundial tile, dated 1765, is presently the only piece attributed to Thomas Greg's first pottery, situated in Little Patrick Street (near present-day Corporation Street). It is also a highly unusual object, being the only known English or Irish delftware sundial and only the second dated tile to be recorded.

to this pottery (Figure 6), a unique manganese-painted delftware sundial tile, made 'For James Reily of Carrickfergus 1765', which bears striking similarity to a class of small, Belfast-made brass sundials of the same date.[42] Documentary information relating to this pottery is meagre, but sufficient to show that it had certainly been working for some time by 1754, that 'Mr Greg' leased the most expensive property on this 'Pot House Lease' in 1763, and that manufacture may have continued into the 1770s. It is therefore possible that the later Downshire Pottery, for Greg, simply represented a dramatic expansion of his prior interests in fine-ceramic manufacture. It is also possible that his first creamware experiments might have been conducted at the Little Patrick Street site, rather than at the later Downshire Pottery.

THE DEVELOPMENT OF BALLYMACARRET

Even if prior experience of ceramics did not contribute directly to the Downshire venture, Thomas Greg certainly recognised the unprecedented commercial opportunities that were offered by the political developments of the early 1780s. Large though the Downshire Pottery was, it actually constituted only one part of a still more ambitious 'grand plan', which Greg (either alone or with others) may have conceived as early as 1782 in direct response to the developing politics. At that time, as the frontispiece shows (see Figure 1), all of what is now east Belfast on the County Down side of the River Lagan was virtually undeveloped. (The area is best known by its townland name of Ballymacarret.) This riverside portion, which faced the quayside of central Belfast, represented a potentially valuable location for new industry, but its unstable tidal shores had prevented building development for well over a century.[43]

The co-ordinated 'grand plan' which Greg appears to have conceived was to develop Ballymacarret by the improbable means of establishing a major glassworks and a fine-pottery there. Apart from the fact that free trade now made these branches of manufacture appear potentially lucrative, Greg recognised that furnace and kiln waste from both industries could be employed as landfill in the immediate vicinity, assisting with land reclamation and generating extra revenue from land sales.[44] In formulating these plans, Greg believed that new, cheap sources of Irish coal were soon due to become available, delivered directly to these riverside industries via the Tyrone and Lagan canals, (which he was also involved in).[45] Furthermore, by establishing a glasshouse and fine-pottery in tandem, machinery and local materials that were essential to both, such as fire-clay, sand, lead ore, manganese and so on, could be utilised with greater efficiency. This would have been of particular advantage to the Downshire Pottery, considering its dependence upon Irish raw materials.

Work on the first of these ventures, the glassworks, was well under way by July 1784.[46] By setting up in glass manufacture first, Greg was able to take advantage of Dublin Society premiums that were already in place for the burgeoning Irish glass industry.[47] As with the later Downshire Pottery, these glassworks were built on an unprecedented scale, incorporating, for example, the largest glass cone ever built in Ireland (and possibly in the entire British Isles). Variously reported at around 120 feet and 150 feet in height, this famous landmark must have represented a potent symbol of Belfast's commercial faith in the liberal political reforms of 1779–82, dominating the town's skyline until 1937 (Figure 7).[48]

By employing Scottish glassmaker John Smylie to manage and supervise the project, building work on the glass cone was complete by August 1785.[49] Three months later, the 'Belfast Glass Company' of John Smylie & Co was formally registered, with Thomas Greg named as the principal of no less than 13 mercantile partners, following which manufacture began in April 1786.[50] Although the glasshouse was unable to achieve full production for a further two years, guards were employed from the outset to ensure that beach gravel, cinders and clinker – which were essential for the land reclamation aspect of this project – were not removed from the vicinity of the glasshouse.[51] Then, with the first stage of his 'grand plan' up and running, Greg turned his attention from establishing the largest glasshouse in Ireland, towards the more difficult matter of setting up the largest pottery in Ireland.

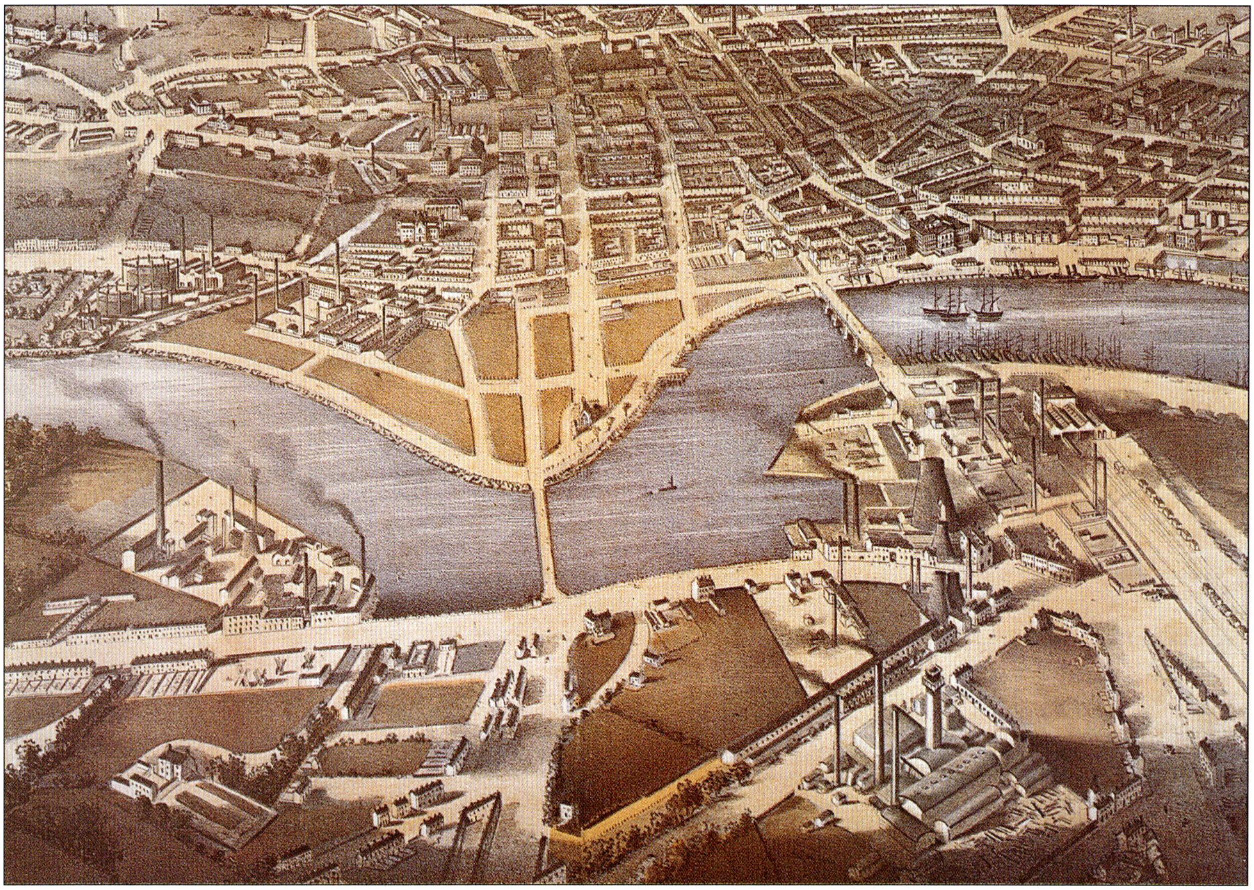

Figure 7. A close-up view of Ballymacarret, as shown in 'A Bird's Eye View of Belfast in 1865', engraving by J H Connop. The large glasshouse of 'Smylie & Co.' is clearly visible on the right, although business had long ceased by 1865. The second 'bottle' glasshouse (built 1792) stood nearby, as did that of Benjamin Edwards. Upstream, (to the left), the kiln of the Downshire Pottery was still visible in 1865, hidden among a profusion of 19th-century industrial buildings. (See also Figure 22, p 20.)

THE FIRST PHASE, 1787–96

Only four days after the editor of the *Belfast News Letter* lamented upon the 'long and injudicious neglect' of pottery and other coal-consuming manufactures in the north of Ireland, notice of intent to establish the Downshire Pottery appeared in the *Dublin Chronicle* on 15 May 1787:[52]

> 'Some gentlemen near Belfast, where are extensive strata of the finest pottery clay, large quantities of which are exported to England, have united for the very laudable purpose of engaging from England some knowing hands and establishing an Irish factory'.

Greg, Stephenson and Ashmore must soon have learned that the 'extensive strata of the finest pottery clay' near Belfast were actually delftware clays, and that clays suitable for creamware were, in reality, extremely rare locally.[53] Despite their flawed optimism, this notice of intent to form the Downshire Pottery in May 1787 provides an obvious commencement date for the venture, but it is more difficult to gauge when creamware manufacture actually began. The tone of the earliest known advertisement for Downshire's 'Cream Colour Ware' five years later (May 1792) implies that the Belfast public were by then already acquainted with their wares.[54] So, without more specific information, the pottery's early history can only be traced indirectly.

Initial progress appears to have been slow, for there is no evidence of any activity at the site on a map drawn up in 1789, but probably surveyed in 1788.[55] The 'China Manufactory' clearly existed in some form by 1790–91, when Williamson's more detailed map was surveyed and published (see frontispiece), but the unfortunate lack of detail with regard to the buildings – presumably indicating that building work was still continuing – makes it difficult to tell whether or not the pottery was capable of working by that stage.[56] Even so, this map usefully highlights the close proximity of Victor Coates' coarse-ware pottery, an independent venture on Downshire's doorstep that made garden pots, tiles and chimney-pots, as well as a 'superior kind of black-glazed ware' (mainly butter-crocks and pans).[57] Coates' kiln-waste may have been similarly employed as landfill in the immediate vicinity, but this has yet to be confirmed by excavation. No examples of his wares are known.

From the scant evidence available, the Downshire Pottery most probably began to manufacture creamware in late 1790 or early 1791, dates which accord most comfortably with the scale of the building works that are now known to have been carried out. By 1791, the author of an 'accurate enumeration' of Belfast was able to state simply that 'here is a manufactory of earthenware', indicating further that earthenware manufacture was one of the new trades which had 'rapidly increased' the town's importance in recent years.[58] A more interesting piece of circumstantial evidence derives from a Mr Reid, a Scottish potter and flint mill owner, who remarked in 1791 that his flints 'were imported from Gravesend' in Kent, to his flint mill, 'from which they went to Glasgow, Ireland, and his own pottery at West-Pans'.[59] This strikes a resonant note of significance in that the Downshire Pottery did not finish building its own flint mill in Belfast (the only one in Ireland) for a further four years (November 1795).[60] Although ground flint was not strictly a prohibited export, considering the difficulty which Downshire may have experienced in obtaining supplies from England directly, this Scottish supplier seems a plausible source.

In view of the initial obstacles that Greg, Stephenson and Ashmore must have overcome it is particularly unfortunate that so little is known of the first few years of their pottery's existence. They left no clues as to where they obtained their white-firing Irish clays, nor do we have any indication of where their potters came from. Some of their early difficulties are alluded to in a later petition to the Irish Parliament (see appendix, p 13), but the first firm indication of the state of progress appeared in March 1792, when Greg, Stephenson and Ashmore described themselves as 'Manufacturers of Queen's Ware' in their first application for Dublin Society aid.[61] Two months later, Downshire's 'Cream Colour Ware' was offered for sale by Belfast's principal china-merchant, James Cleland, who remarked upon their wares in a small footnote to his announcement that he had just imported 'from London and Paris... a new and elegant assortment of East India and French porcelain... and Stafford Shire Ware'.[62] Rather than loudly proclaiming the new, local creamware as might be expected, Cleland's advertisement more forcefully demonstrates the daunting foreign competition that Downshire faced from the outset, even in its home town. An editorial which appeared in the *Belfast News Letter* a few days later on 15 June 1792 conveys more obvious local pride and demonstrates the close links between the pottery and Smylie's Glassworks.[63]

> ... Ireland, particularly in the town and neighbourhood of Belfast, has of late years made considerable progress in some of the most valuable [manufacturing industries]. As fire-clay and sand are essential materials in making GLASS and FINE POTTERY-WARE, gentlemen finding these on their estates would serve their country by sending samples of either, to Messrs. John Smylie & Co., proprietors of the new Glass-house, or Messrs. Greg, Stephenson, and Ashmore, proprietors of the Pottery; to this they will be induced by patriotism, independently of emolument. In addition to the lately established manufactures above mentioned, we are happy to find that the foundation of a Bottle Glass-House, on the largest scale, has been laid by Messrs. John Smylie & Co., when finished, we shall have three glass-houses [in Belfast] where within these few years there was not one.

This announcement of the foundation of a bottle glasshouse by Smylie & Co (once again, the largest in Ireland) is important for two reasons.[64] First, it shows that there was still sufficient confidence in these industries for a new and ambitious project to be undertaken as late as June 1792, only five years before the pottery and both of Smylie's glasshouses failed. Second, if Greg retained only one 'construction-team' for both, then this expansion of the glassworks could mean that building work at the pottery was substantially completed at about that time.

By this stage (June 1792), Greg, Stephenson and Ashmore had already borne the exceptional cost of establishing the Downshire Pottery for a full five years without Dublin Society aid, and even then, some further building work was still required.[65] In addition, there appear to have been initial problems with the quality of the creamware they were developing, which must have added to the financial burden. It is perhaps not surprising, therefore, to find that Greg, Stephenson and Ashmore set about raising some cash. In September, they sold a small but valuable plot of built-up land in the vicinity of the pottery – perhaps even a part of the pottery itself – which brought them the very substantial sum of £700.[66] (The prominent buy-back clause in this agreement suggests that the sale was intended as a temporary, cash-raising expedient – rather than the sale of newly-reclaimed land, for example.) Whether as a result of these funds or for other reasons, the problems with their creamware seem to have been resolved within months, as their second advertisement in the local press indicates (November 1792).[67]

> POTTERY, BALLYMACARRET, near BELFAST. GREG, STEPHENSON and ASHMORE, after various disappointments, have brought the Manufacture of Cream-coloured or Queen's Earthen-Ware to a Degree of Perfection much superior to what it was. They have now ready for Sale, a large Assortment of Blue, Painted and Cream-coloured Ware, which they will sell on such Terms, as they hope will encourage Shopkeepers and others in the Trade to favour them with their Commands.

The early difficulties with the creamware quality may relate to two obvious defects which were found to exist among the surviving Downshire wares; over-firing (producing a ware resembling an unevenly-glazed, white, salt-glazed stoneware) and disfiguring, brown glaze-spots, reminiscent of heavy sprinklings of pepper (see Figure 28). Two months later again, the Downshire partnership attempted to increase the level of government funding by appealing directly to the Irish Parliament for aid. Their petition (see appendix, p 13)

Figure 8. This early 19th-century view of Belfast was painted by Hugh Fraser from the northern edge of Victor Coates' pottery, a viewpoint of the town that was not available before the potteries were built. While the Downshire Pottery buildings are not illustrated, the proximity of the related glasshouses and the general character of Ballymacarret at the time are evident.

was successful, for three days later it was resolved that they 'deserved the aid of Parliament', although this additional aid ultimately amounted to only £40 a year in hard cash.[68]

It seems that as soon as Greg, Stephenson and Ashmore had resolved one difficulty, another arose to take its place. In a letter of gratitude (2 February 1793) to the pottery's patron, the Marquess of Downshire, (acknowledging his assistance in obtaining this parliamentary aid the day before),[69] Greg mentions a new problem:

> I gratefully thank your Lordship for your active and so far successful exertions to procure aid to the infant Downshire manufacture... I have had it in contemplation to prepare, and still have, a set with your Lordship's arms or the initial letters of your name on it, but am prevented for want of a good painter, a great loss to the manufacture; there is one, a private in the 70th Regiment, who would answer the purpose completely, but notwithstanding repeated applications to Lt-Col. Coote, he cannot be prevailed on either to grant him a long furlough, nor a discharge... There is a distressing circumstance, the company had taken four or five apprentices who were in a few days making considerable progress under Tho. Davis Bayley's care and are idle since his departure: that is the name of the private I wish to be discharged...[70]

These references to crested and monogrammed creamware decoration suggest that Thomas Davis-Bayley was a fine-quality painter in overglaze enamels, and this letter suggests that Downshire had not developed this form of decoration to any extent by February 1793. In turn, this might help to explain the poor calligraphy and spelling on an overglaze-enamelled Belfast teapot (See colour plate 15, p40, right), which has been attributed to Downshire by the style of the enamelling and the moulded spout. The 70th regiment was one of many English regiments that were then garrisoned in Belfast, but, as early 1793 was an especially sensitive time politically, (England entered into war with France, and Irish Volunteer regiments were disbanded) Greg might well have experienced difficulty in securing Davis-Bayley's discharge for several months afterwards.[71] For whatever reason, Downshire does not appear to have resumed its advertisements of 'painted earthen-ware' until November, 10 months later.

Otherwise, 1793 seems to have been a year of steady improvement. For most of the year they offered for sale 'a large assortment of Blue, Cream and other coloured Earthen-Ware, of the best qualities...' at prices 'much lower than the like can be imported for'.[72] (These advertisements probably refer to pearlwares, creamwares, and creamwares with a coloured slip.) By

November, it also appears that the quality of the wares had been improved still further, as their advertisement in that month stated that they now offered 'a great variety of cream-coloured and painted earthen-ware, which they can assure their friends and customers, is of the best quality, and NOW equal to any imported'.[73] The pottery also supplied apothecaries with 'any quantity of GALLIPOTS', and they had also manufactured sufficient 'well-ground manganese' (glaze pigment) to offer a surplus for sale.[74]

At this point, just when Downshire's operations finally appear to have started running smoothly, their local newspaper advertisements virtually cease, probably because demand for Downshire's wares at this time exceeded their ability to supply. By 1794, their creamwares were very likely precisely as stated: 'equal to' and 'cheaper than' imported creamwares, so that their business appears to have thrived. In November 1794, Greg, Stephenson and Ashmore applied for a further extension to their Dublin Society aid, while the following May they advertised simply that they were selling 'cream-coloured and painted earthenware'.[75] In November 1795, Greg finished building his 'flint mill... necessary for Earthen Ware', submitting his Dublin Society claim accordingly.[76] However, although it appears that Downshire had finally brought their difficulties under control, a closer look at their Dublin Society premiums makes it evident that the pottery's output fell dramatically towards the end of this period. Whereas *annual production* had been valued at £1045.4s 3d and £1107.14s. respectively in their first two years of claims (June 1792 – May 1794), the value of their total production for the *22 months* between 1 June 1794 and 31 March 1796 was only £1001.6.s 11.d[77]

This dramatic decline in the pottery's fortunes was almost certainly connected with the death of Thomas Greg, at the age of 78, on 10 January 1796.[78] The clearest evidence that Greg represented the vital driving force behind these precarious pottery and glassmaking ventures is the speed with which they collapsed after his demise. The Downshire Pottery appears to have ceased production almost immediately, as demonstrated by the premature termination of Dublin Society premiums on 31 March 1796, while potentially a more final note was struck in August when the flint mill was sold to another wealthy Belfast family, the Stevensons.[79] In 1798, shortly before Victor Coates also closed down his affiliated coarse-ware pottery, a visitor to the town observed that the attempt 'to introduce a similar fabric to that of Wedgwood... has been given up for some time'.[80]

Even Smylie & Co's glassworks failed only a year after Greg's death, despite the fact that Greg had been incorporated with a large consortium of highly capable merchants in this more secure industry. Although Smylie & Co successfully gained additional revenue from the sale of reclaimed land, as had been planned from the outset, the cost of building glassworks on such a scale appears to have left their finances in an unhealthy state.[81] In April 1797, just a few days before extension of the excise duty to Ireland would have placed further burden on their finances, Smylie & Co began to sell off materials and equipment.[82] Thereafter, this 'largest glass-cone in Ireland' never worked to capacity again, though it was revived in more subdued fashion after 1800, (like the Downshire Pottery itself).[83]

Such were the complexities of Thomas Greg's business affairs that his eldest son, Cunningham Greg (Figure 9), spent several years afterwards settling his father's estate. In February 1799, Cunningham first bought out all of the remaining partners in Smylie & Co's glassworks, confirming that Thomas Greg had borne principal responsibility for the venture.[84] In October the same year, the Downshire Pottery was finally wound up with this advertisement in the *Belfast News Letter* on 29 October 1799.[85]

> PARTNERSHIP DISSOLVED. The Partnership formerly subsisting under the firm of Greg, Stephenson, and Ashmore, has been for some time dissolved. Any demands against the said Partnership will be paid by applying to Cunningham Greg, [S.] M. Stephenson & John Ashmore.

The Revival of the Pottery, 1800–c.1806

While Belfast now possessed a brand new, 'Staffordshire-type' pottery, the 1799 notice clearly indicates that it remained closed for several years after Greg's death. This period of inactivity coincides broadly with the turbulent events which preceded and accompanied the 1798 rebellion; an episode which invoked sharp economic recession throughout Ireland during 1797–98, and which had some especially severe effects in Belfast.[86] As any subsequent revival of the Downshire Pottery probably involved substantial financial outlay it is perhaps not surprising to find that no new investor came forward until the political situation had stabilised. With the approach of the much-debated union between England and Ireland, however, which finally took effect from 1 January 1801, the economic climate recovered steadily through 1799 and 1800.

There is little doubt that some form of revival took place at the pottery during the early years of the 19th century, probably from late 1800–c.1806, but for the present, documentary evidence is extremely scant. Almost certainly, the pottery enterprise was carried on in a much reduced form, for if a full staff had been brought in again after three and a half years of closure there would almost certainly have been much more fanfare associated with its re-opening. As it is, were it not for one trade directory entry and a single newspaper advertisement, there would be no certainty that the revival happened at all.

The first indication that the pottery was again working dates from December 1800, (three weeks before the Act of Union was due to come into effect), when the following advertisement appeared in the *Belfast News Letter*:

> *JAMES AND WILLIAM TENNANT, MANUFACTURERS OF STAFFORDSHIRE EARTHENWARE* Most respectfully inform their Friends and the Public, that they have opened a Wholesale and Retail Warehouse, opposite Mr.

Figure 9. Thomas Greg at home with his family, c.1765–70. Greg's eldest son Cunningham, who closed down the Downshire Pottery in 1799, is on the extreme right of the picture. A younger son Samuel, the founder of the Quarry Bank Mill at Styal in Cheshire, stands at his father's elbow.

Figure 10. Thomas Greg's tomb, (centre left), today stands in disrepair in the grounds of Knockbreda Church, alongside that of his lifelong friend Waddell Cunningham. This early 19th-century watercolour by Andrew Nicholl gives a clear impression of the memorial's original aspect, overlooking the pottery, glasshouses and other ventures in Belfast that Greg had spent his life creating.

> Edwards' Foundry, at the Bridge end, where Shopkeepers and Hawkers may be supplied upon the most reasonable terms. N.B. Gentlemen's Table Services compleat, of different patterns and best quality.[87]

Even though mention is only made of a 'Wholesale and Retail Warehouse' close to the Downshire Pottery (opposite Mr Edwards' 'New Foundry' – see frontispiece), this advertisement almost certainly announces the re-opening of the pottery, funded once more by members of a well-established family within the upper echelons of Belfast's closely-knit merchant community, whose frequently misspelt surname was *Tennent*.[88] The early Belfast historian George Benn indicated that the individuals involved were indeed this Belfast family, despite the confusing spelling, while FJ Bigger went further – recording that the venture continued until 1805.[89] Unfortunately, it has not been possible to find the evidence upon which he based this assertion.

There is a good reason for being pedantic in trying to establish that the Belfast Tennents were indeed the family involved in attempting to resuscitate the pottery. William Tennent later went on to become one of the most influential merchants in 19th-century Belfast, even founding a bank, so he seems a good candidate for restarting the pottery, but at the time the advertisement appeared in 1800 he was interned in Scotland as a consequence of his involvement in the uprising in 1798. While in prison, it seems that several of his various businesses (such as his sugar house, for example) were kept running by partners, so that if this was the same William Tennent who re-opened the pottery, he could only have been lending financial support to the venture initially. The belief that this was the William Tennent involved is further strengthened by the fact that the existing owner, Cunningham Greg, was in 1798 perceived by the English Commander, Major General Nugent, as having strong sympathies with the United Irishmen. This suggests that in addition to being merchants of roughly equivalent commercial stature, Greg and Tennent might well have shared political views and were possibly well acquainted.[90]

So far, the best corroborating evidence to show that the pottery started up again after 1800 has come from Belfast's earliest trade directory, which in its editorial remarked in 1805 upon the town's 'considerable manufactures of cotton, cambric, sail cloth, and linen, with others of glass, sugar, *earthen-ware*... &c.'[91]

Further supporting evidence derives from the wares themselves, some of which appear to be later in date than 1800. For example, the overtly 'Irish' moulded–border design of shamrocks and harps (Figure 11), which also occurs on the zebra and stag-painted plates shown (colour plates 18 and 19), is too stylistically complex to date from c.1791–96 but would neatly fit the early 19th century. Similarly, some small helmet-shaped pearlware jugs, two of which have turned up in Belfast, are painted with a harp and shamrock on each side (Figure 12). As can be seen, almost precisely the same design was also produced on glass decanters made by Benjamin Edwards in Ballymacarret during the early years of the 19th century.

The *Belfast Trade Directory* for 1807 shows that the Downshire property was occupied primarily by the Vitriol Works of Cunningham Greg and William Boyd from that time onwards, suggesting that the pottery had closed at some time between 1805 and 1807, and that ownership of the site had again reverted to Greg. There is a chance that the pottery might still have existed in some form, even at that date, although the chance is admittedly slim.[92] Overall, the paucity of firm information regarding the second phase of the Downshire Pottery is reminiscent of the situation in Dublin 20 years before, where the World's End pottery's early activity (during the 'high-profile' years of Stacey & Co) is fairly well known, but much more obscure afterwards. Without some new documentary evidence, this second phase of the pottery's activity in Belfast will remain equally undefined.

One new potential line of enquiry comes from a more recent discovery, concerning another Belfast man, James Stevenson, who soon afterwards became a co-founder of the Clyde and Ladyburn (creamware) potteries in Greenock in 1815. The Stevensons were once again a well-known Belfast family of the time, though not quite on a par with merchants such as Greg and Tennent.[93] In 1796, we find that the Downshire Pottery's essential flint mill was sold to this Stevenson family in Belfast, which could even suggest that they had bought an interest in the venture, as there are not many uses for a flint mill except in making pottery and glass.[94] Before this Greenock Pottery connection was found, it was assumed that ownership of the flint mill ultimately ended up with one of the local glassworks – a James Stevenson was listed, in fact, as one of the investors in Smylie's glassworks, but looking again at the 1791 map (see frontispiece) we can also see that the Stevenson family home was a large estate situated right alongside the Downshire Pottery itself (the area shown as Mount Pottinger and Mr Cunningham's).[95] There is obviously more to this connection than presently meets the eye. James Stevenson is known to have been listed in a Glasgow trade directory from 1809 onwards as a china and stoneware merchant, but whether he was fully resident in Glasgow or in Belfast is not clear. In 1816, for example, he is listed in Belfast trade directories as a retailer of Scottish pottery.

For the present therefore, it is simply not clear how long the Downshire Pottery lasted after 1800, nor can we guess the extent to which it was revived. It seems reasonably certain that the pottery operated from 1800 to 1805 or 1806 under the ownership of James and William Tennent but thereafter the details become hazy. James Stevenson, who later became involved in pottery manufacture in Glasgow, was almost certainly associated with the revival in some way – his family were in possession of the vital flint mill from 1796, after all. But for now, Stevenson's connection actually muddies the waters further, because presumably he also made some wares in Scotland for the Irish market, which he then would have sold in Belfast. This might well cause difficulties when we try to attribute early 19th-century wares to Downshire. Sadly, because the excavated shards

Figure 11. Oval creamware dish border. Four of these plain white dishes have turned up in Belfast in recent years. The border style suggests an early 19th-century date so that, if these dishes were locally produced, they must have been produced during the Downshire Pottery's second phase of activity, after 1800.

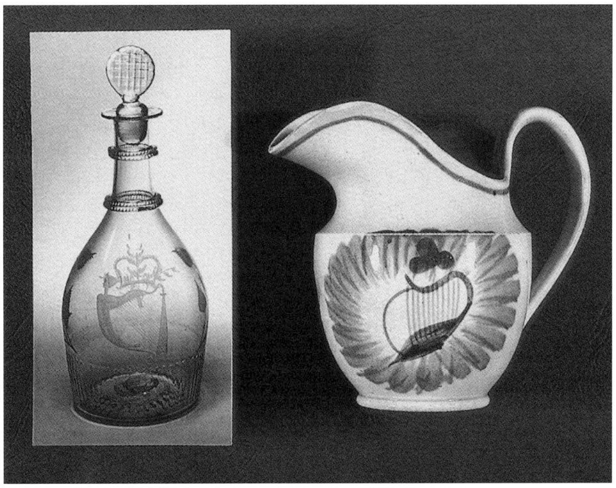

Figure 12. The decanter on the left was made at Benjamin Edwards' glasshouse in Ballymacarret during the early 1800s. A similar harp and shamrock design appears on a group of small, pearlware jugs (right) that are tentatively attributed to the second phase of the Downshire Pottery's operation, after 1800.

recovered all appear to date from 1793 or before they are of no help in recognising the post-1800 wares. For now, the final phase of the Downshire Pottery's history and the wares that were made then must remain among its best kept secrets.

APPENDIX

Greg, Stephenson and Ashmore's petition to the Irish Parliament, 1 February 1793:

> To the Right Honourable and Honourable the Knights, Citizens and Burgesses in Parliament assembled: The Humble Petition of Thomas Greg, Samuel Stephenson, and John Ashmore, of Belfast. Sheweth that your Petitioners, taking into consideration the many and great advantages which might arise from the Introduction of a Manufacture of Queen's Ware, and other kinds of fine Earthen Ware, such as made in Staffordshire. They conceived that Many Materials which have been heretofore overlooked and neglected would be thus rendered useful and important, and many Workmen and Children would thus find Employment. With these Views, and from these Motives, your Petitioners have united themselves into a Company, and, by their Exertions, have carried this Manufacture to greater Perfection, in the County of Down, near Belfast, than was ever known in this Kingdom. Your Petitioners have been at great Expence in searching for and making Experiments upon Materials for this Purpose, the most important of which they have discovered in this Country, and which are mostly prohibited from being imported from England. Your Petitioners have also been at great Expence in erecting Buildings, in importing Machinery, and in bringing Workmen from foreign Places. Your Petitioners have found that the Expence attending the Introduction of this new Manufacture, and Difference in the Price of Coals from what they are in Staffordshire, has greatly exceeded their Expectations, and that several additional Buildings are necessary to the greater Extent and Perfection of it.
>
> For these Reasons your Petitioners do humbly hope this Honourable House will take this Matter under Consideration and grant such Aid as shall seem meet... [signed by Greg, Stephenson and Ashmore].
>
> (PRONI T/533/5)

The Pottery Site

Previous Research

As we have seen there are many gaps in the history of Downshire Pottery, but thanks to the 1791 map (see frontispiece) there has never been any doubt about its location. Finds of pottery were first recorded on the site by the Belfast historian RM Young as long ago as 1896, when several of the surviving pottery buildings, such as the kiln, were demolished to make way for a new distillery.[96] Young had visited this 'interesting site' some years previously without finding signs of Downshire's wares, but in consequence of the building work he discovered 'at a depth of four feet from the present surface, associated with fragments of earthenware seggars… many specimens of a coarse porcelain (creamware biscuit)… in the form of broken cups, saucers, bowls, teapots, &c.' Three of Young's shards were illustrated by Dudley Westropp in 1913 (Figure 13), sufficient to show that these waster deposits were identical in character to those found again a century later.[97]

Figure 13. Three creamware shards found by RM Young on the Downshire Pottery site in 1896, together with a jelly mould which he believed was made in Belfast (bottom left). This illustration first appeared in a paper presented to the Royal Irish Academy by MSD Westropp in 1913.

Figure 14. The layer of broken pottery waste on the Downshire Pottery site, as first encountered in June 1993.

The excavations

In June 1993, the fact that construction work was just beginning on the privately-owned Downshire Pottery site prompted the author to request permission to investigate further. At that early stage, there were only some deep foundation holes, but these at least afforded an opportunity to look for signs of pottery waste beneath the layers of concrete and tarmac that overlie much of the area. Disappointingly, nothing was visible, (even at RM Young's recommended depth of three to four feet), except for one or two white traces at the bottom of one of the holes that *might* have been pottery clay. Consequently, the investigations very nearly ceased at this point.

With the owner's help, however, a small mechanical digger was brought in to deepen the hole and explore further. Almost immediately, the digger's shovel penetrated through into a solid pocket of broken pottery waste half a metre thick, comprised almost entirely of fragments of delicate objects such as bowls, plates and teapots, amongst large lumps of clinker and 'kiln furniture' (Figure 14). For the first time since RM Young made his finds on the site in 1896, it was possible to actually handle pieces of Downshire Pottery.

The area in which the finds were encountered was due to be covered with reinforced concrete flooring in

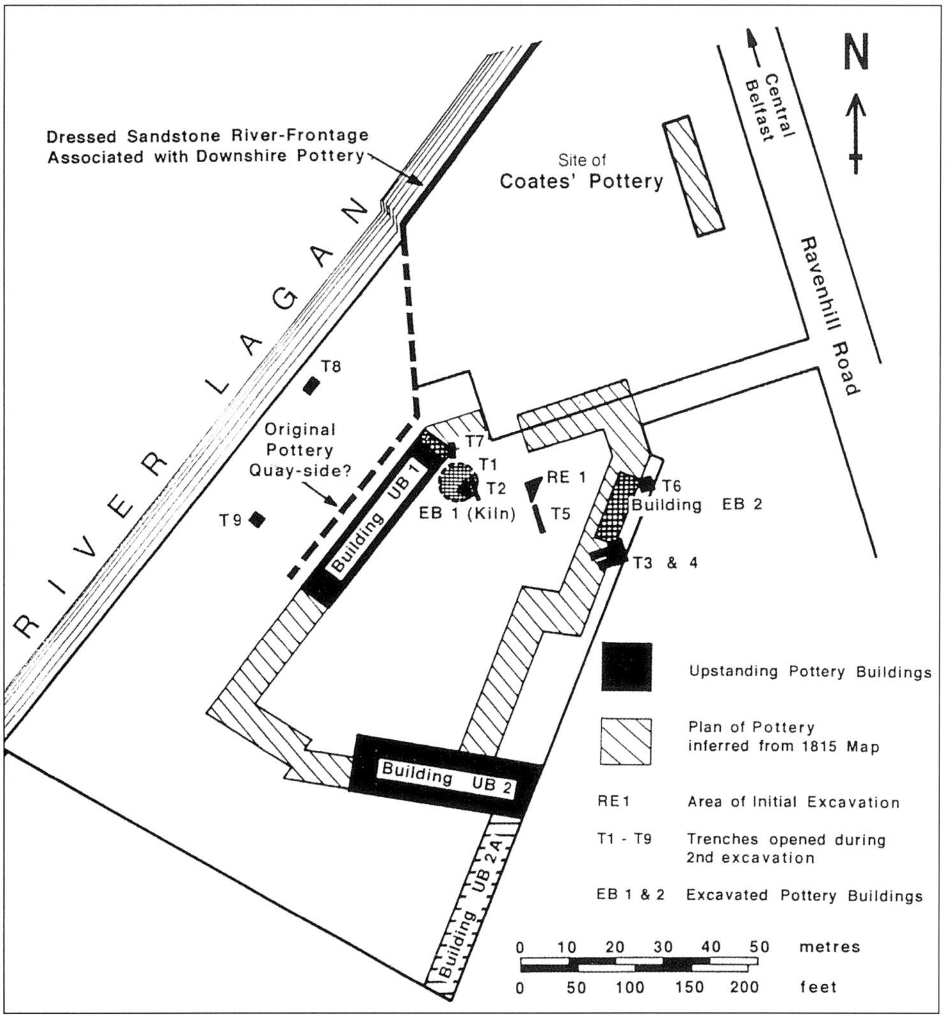

Figure 15. A plan of the 1993 Downshire excavations. Also shown are the positions of the standing pottery buildings, and details taken from an 1815 map of the site.

a matter of days, to support the installation of a pressurised gas vessel. Large quantities of pottery fragments were obviously present, and so this deadline in turn prompted the first 'excavation' of the site – a rescue excavation (prefixed on maps and descriptions by the letters RE). With the help of Professor Mike Baillie of Queen's University Belfast, Felicity Graham and some interested members of a university evening class, the entire deposit of pottery fragments – some 50 centimetres in thickness and covering an area of 10 square metres – was retrieved within the next three days, ahead of the builder's schedule.[98] (See Figure 15. The area that was first excavated is indicated as Trench RE1.) During the next few weeks, the finds that were collected were washed and sorted, yielding in total about 50 kilograms of pottery fragments, (which are now incorporated in the Ulster Museum's collection). It was later to transpire that this relatively small, isolated pocket of material actually constituted the most useful and informative pottery assemblage found anywhere on the site, because it contained a higher than usual percentage of the most distinctive, coloured and decorated fragments.[99]

It is also worth remarking at this point that this initial 'rescue dig' was by no means an archaeological excavation in the truest sense. Rather than slowly examining and removing the layer of interest with a trowel as archaeologists prefer, to gain most information and cause least damage, the pottery was simply dug out using a mechanical shovel, then sorted and bagged on surface. Given the time constraints, this was the only possible means of recovering the most significant material, the pottery fragments themselves. Even so, material was removed in an ordered fashion, using a metre-square gridded system, and sections were recorded. Had time been available, however, a more cautious approach would have yielded better results, and caused less damage to the fragments.

This first rescue 'excavation' ended as soon as the small pocket of pottery wasters was fully exhausted, but

Figure 16. Archaeologist Tom McErlean studying the fully excavated Downshire Pottery kiln (see Figure 19).

because it was now possible to investigate the site directly a still more remarkable discovery was made: two of the original Downshire Pottery buildings were still standing (Figure 15, Buildings UB1 and 2. See also Figure 22). In combination with 1833 edition Ordnance Survey maps, these buildings allowed the position of the pottery's free-standing kiln – the most important structure on the site – to be pinpointed, but most of this area was already under concrete by the time it was located. Just one small part of the kiln remained clear, and even this was due for destruction within the following two months, as building work progressed.[100]

As the kiln site was under threat, the Environment and Heritage Service kindly made available the funds necessary for a small, formal excavation on the Downshire site; the first excavation of an 18th-century fine-pottery in Ireland. The principal aim of this 14-day investigation during August/September 1993 was to record the last remaining portion of the kiln before its destruction, but the investigations actually managed to achieve very much more. In addition to a thoroughly successful kiln-excavation (Figures 16 and 19), a further eight trenches were opened up (Figure 17. See also Figure 15, Trenches T1–9). This revealed an otherwise unrecorded pottery building (Building EB2) and established the stratigraphy of the pottery deposits over a large area. Only one section is shown here (Figure 21, Trenches 3–4, the longest section recorded), but this is sufficient to demonstrate that pottery waste actually formed an almost continuous layer that was originally deposited by the potters right across the site, presumably to improve the quality of the muddy, 'green-field' ground surface on which the Downshire Pottery was situated.

Figure 17. Trench 4, which provided most of the biscuit-ware fragments recovered, in the process of excavation by Laura Francis, Melanie Reid, Nick Lewis and Vaughn Gibson.

The nine exploratory trenches shown in Figure 15 (p 15) can be summarised briefly as follows:

Trench 1: an exploratory narrow trench, which helped to locate the position of the kiln precisely and determine whether its foundations had survived.

Trench 2: the kiln excavation (Figures 16 and 19. For further discussion, see p 19, The Buildings).

Trench 3: (see Figure 21, p 19).This began as the largest trial trench that was undertaken, sited in an area which builder's foundation holes suggested might be rich in pottery waste. In the event, the trench encountered the corner of a large stone-built building that must once have been part of the original Downshire Pottery complex. (For further discussion, see p 19, The Buildings.)

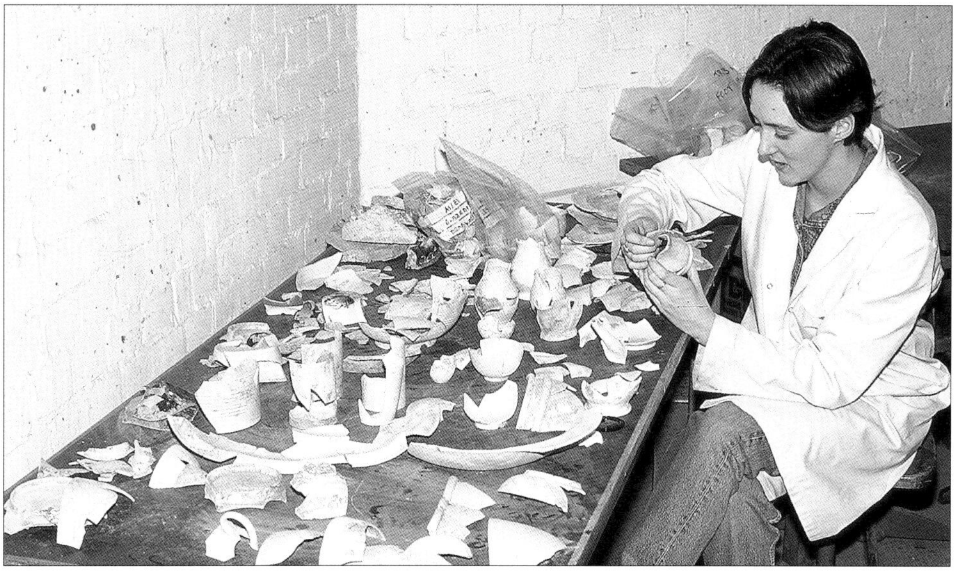

Figure 18. Post-excavation washing and sorting. Linda Canning with a small sample of the thousands of fragments which were examined in the course of preparing this catalogue.

Trench 4: (see Figure 21, p 19). One side of Trench 3 was found to contain a thick deposit of pottery waste, and so Trench 4 was excavated away from this point to determine how far the pottery waste extended. It was from here that the majority of the Downshire Pottery fragments were recovered. (See Figure 17.)

Trench 5: a small, opportunistic trench near the original 'rescue excavation', which unsuccessfully attempted to find similar pottery deposits, with a relatively high percentage of decorated wares.

Trench 6: a very small trench, which pinpointed the location of the opposite corner of the building encountered in Trench 3, to test the accuracy of the early maps of the site.

Trench 7: an unsuccessful attempt to locate the original corner of the best-preserved remaining building. The area is criss-crossed with buried cables and pipes.

Trenches 8 and 9: land on this side of the Downshire Pottery, towards the River Lagan, has obviously been built up with around two to three metres of landfill since the time of the pottery. These two, widely-spaced trial trenches were excavated to determine whether this area had been built up using discarded pottery waste, but this was not the case. Even at the old beach level (at the bottom), no significant traces of pottery were found.

In total, the nine trenches excavated provided some 350 kilograms of ceramic kiln-waste (of which c.250 kilograms proved to be saggar fragments, the majority of which were not kept).[101] In 1995–96, with the help of Ulster Museum funding, this collection of pottery waste was painstakingly washed and sorted by Linda Canning at the Institute of Irish Studies, Queen's University Belfast (Figure 18 above).

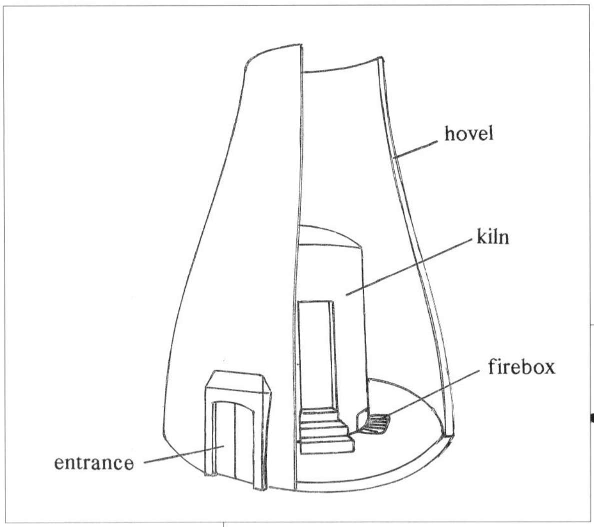

Figure 20. A cross section of a typical bottle oven. As the 'Bird's Eye View' of 1865 shows, however (Figure 22), the Downshire Pottery hovel was more conical than 'bottle-shaped', and was probably 55–65 feet in height.

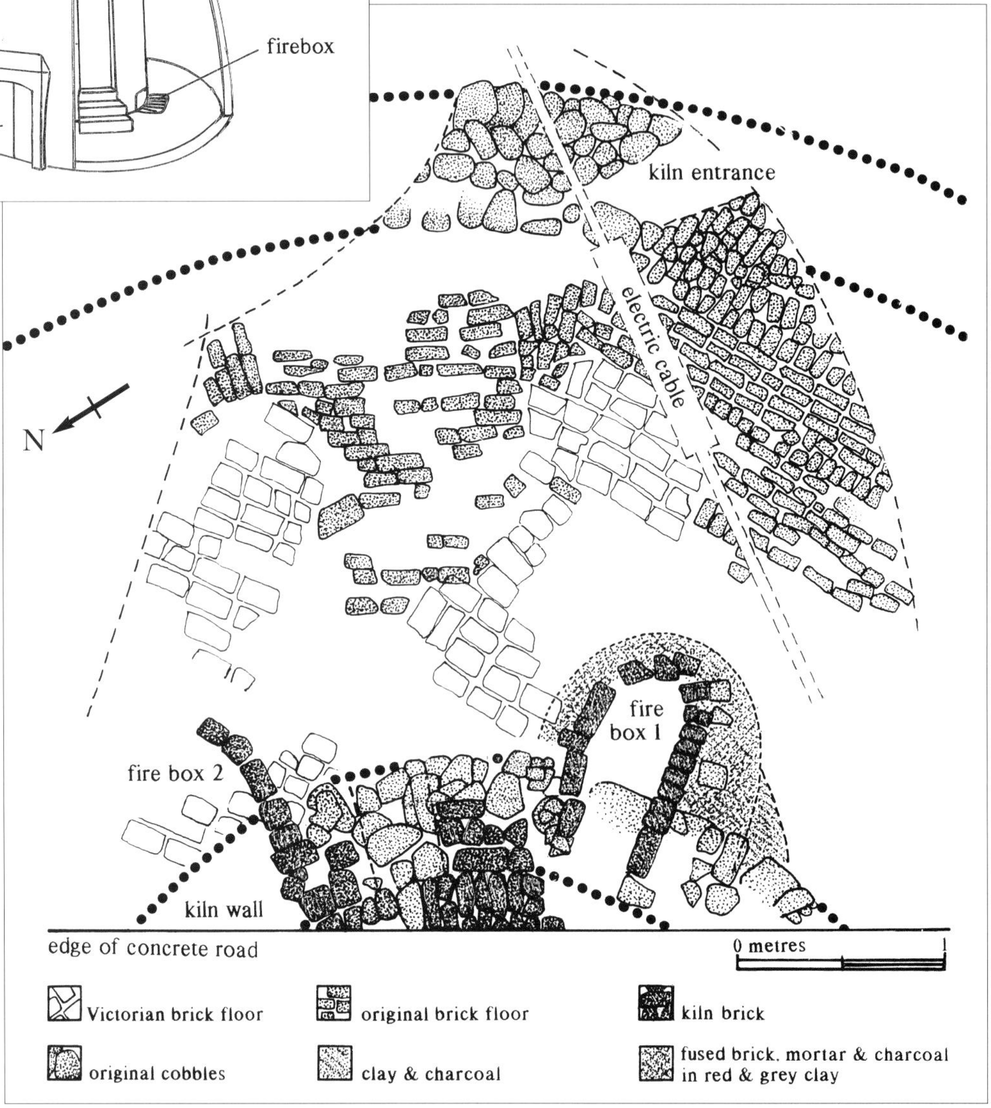

Figure 19. Downshire kiln plan. Only a small portion of the original kiln was found to survive, but this was sufficient to show that the inner 'oven' or kiln proper was slightly larger than most English kilns of that date (15 feet internal diameter. This kiln was set inside a well-built conical 'hovel' 36 feet in diameter). Two firemouths and ashpits were also encountered, (in which the fire was set), indicating that there were probably six firemouths originally. The wide area of brick floor between oven and hovel showed extensive signs of heat-damage and many patches of repair, which suggests that the kiln was used over a considerable period of time. To the top right, it can be seen that the brick floor extends across the hovel wall, indicating that this was the location of the original entrance.

Illustration by Deirdre Crone, Ulster Museum

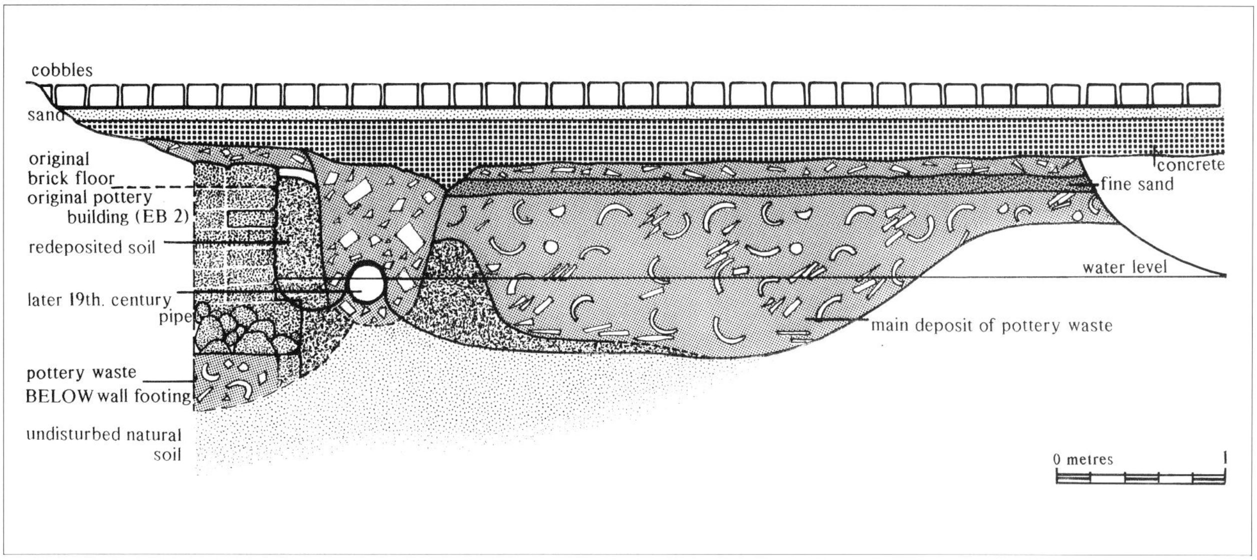

Figure 21. Schematic section of Trench 4. This section gives a clear impression of the stratigraphy of the deposits that overlay most of the pottery site. A deposit of pottery waste ranging from 0.3 to 1.6 metres in thickness was deposited directly onto natural soil, rather in the fashion of 'hard core' or gravel, to first level out the site. (This also proves that the kiln was working at an early stage, to provide these very large quantities of waste.) The foundations of the pottery building discovered by the excavation (left hand side) were also underlain by kiln waste, indicating that the kiln was in operation before this building was erected. Later pottery fragments were also recovered inside the building, on the old floor level.

The only area in which this levelling layer of pottery waste was not found was on the River Lagan side of the pottery buildings, where the quayside was kept clean and free from obstruction. During the 19th century, and some time after the pottery had ceased work, a layer of sharp sand was put down over the entire site as a base for basalt 'square-sets' or cobbles. This re-surfacing most likely occurred during the 1870s when the area was regenerated as Cromac Distillery.

The Buildings

In June 1993, the discovery that an unrecorded and seemingly anonymous old warehouse building was in fact a part of the original Downshire Pottery itself, provided the rarest of archaeological opportunities: a chance to look up, rather than down.

More than any other aspect of these investigations, this discovery – which in time showed that not just one but *two* of the original Downshire Pottery buildings had survived to the present day – emphasised the epic scale of the venture which Greg, Stephenson and Ashmore embarked upon in 1787. Apart from one passing comment in 1837, that the pottery had been built 'upon a very large scale', all of the available evidence had suggested that this was a small, almost experimental pottery, employing perhaps 20 or 30 people at most.[102] With the rediscovery of the buildings, however, it immediately became apparent that the true figure employed there was probably much greater, for the standing remains alone could very comfortably have accommodated a workforce of 120–150 persons, quite possibly many more.

Besides representing the only purpose-built, 18th-century 'Staffordshire-type' pottery in Ireland, these beautifully-made, red Scrabo sandstone warehouses are now among the last surviving 18th-century buildings in Belfast, exhibiting a host of architectural features not found in any other local context. The 'bird's eye view' of the site in 1865 (Figure 22), gives a better impression of the Downshire Pottery's original appearance than can readily be gained today, and we can recognise the two buildings which still stand.[103]

Looking more closely at the site, there are in fact three main elements of the pottery remaining, only two of which are buildings, but all robustly constructed of high-quality, dressed and slate-spaced Scrabo sandstone (rather than the usual brick). This fine-quality masonry in itself shows that the pottery was a major investment, built with unusual pride and built to last. The least obvious of the three features is the sandstone quayside and a 75-metre stretch of river-wall that is still visible alongside the river Lagan today (Figure 23). This substantial river-wall was originally much longer, probably enclosing a large part of the promontory on which the Downshire Pottery was situated (probably as far north as the lime kilns indicated on the 1791 map, see frontispiece). Once again, this reinforces the scale of the task which Greg & Co undertook, considering that all of this river-wall would probably have been built at a cost *additional* to that of the Downshire Pottery itself. From the excavations, it now seems that the site was probably developed by first building this wall along the river's edge, then back-filling with earth on the landward side while simultaneously building the pottery, and finally levelling out the site with kiln-waste.

The best-preserved of the pottery buildings is a 130-feet long, two-storey shed (Building UB1, Figure 15), originally situated with the pottery's quay on one side and the kiln on the other.[104] Figure 24 illustrates the condition of the building at the time of the excavation, when it was being used as a warehouse. Both sides of the ground floor were originally punctuated along their length by numerous archways (more clearly seen in the measured drawing shown in Figure 25), suggesting that this building was a straightforward loading and unloading facility for both quayside and kiln, although it is possible that clay milling also took place there at the southern end. The building has undoubtedly had a hard life in its two centuries of continual use. The internal first floor has been taken out, while the original roof was burned off at some time around 1900 (to be replaced with possibly the last remaining 'Belfast Roof' in Belfast). The ground level has also risen about two feet since the pottery was built, so that the ground floor archways now seem unusually low. But this remains a fine building, one which could readily be restored if opportunity arose. A factor that would make such a project all the more worthwhile is that the Downshire Pottery's original 18th-century quayside has almost certainly been preserved on the Lagan-facing side of this building, buried underneath the wide yard that now separates it from the river's edge.[105]

The larger of the two surviving buildings (Building UB2, Figure 15), which seems to have housed the main potting and decorating rooms, is more problematic. Two hundred years of continual industrial use has so greatly modified its appearance that a detailed survey would be necessary to identify all of the original features, and it is probably well beyond restoration, even at this stage. Nonetheless, its basic dimensions are impressive: 153 feet long, 43 feet broad and 72 feet high at the apex. Perhaps the most poignant vestige of the original Downshire Pottery are the traces of the large windows that appear to have run all along the south-facing side (Figure 26, p 22), which presumably was where many of the potters and decorators must once have worked to catch as much daylight as possible (Figure 27). The length of the building is presumably orientated east-west for this reason.

Apart from the standing remains, the excavation provided evidence of two further structures. Most important by far was the kiln. This appears to have been of a fairly standard 'Staffordshire-type', although more conical in appearance than standard 'bottle-kilns' (Figures 19, 20 and 22). In this type of kiln the relatively small inner oven (the 'kiln' proper), which sits directly over a brick furnace, is enclosed within the much larger cone-shaped 'hovel' – which acts in effect as a chimney. The hovel was especially well constructed, with foundations two feet in thickness made of finely 'dressed' basalt blocks (presumably the hovel walls changed to brick above ground level). Within this outer hovel, around the oven, the entire structure was filled with a basal deposit of very fine, impermeable, red clay – purposely laid to prevent the kiln drawing water from the underlying water-table when it was firing. (The phenomenon is properly termed 'coning-up'. The clouds of steam which resulted frequently damaged the kiln or – more catastrophically – caused it to explode.) Over this lay a one foot thick bed of sand, on which the brick working-floor in turn and the brick oven foundations were laid.

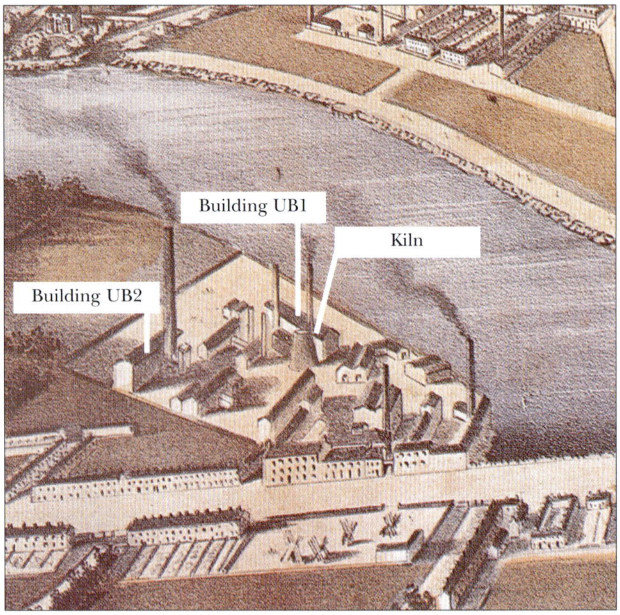

Figure 22. A greatly enlarged view of the Downshire Pottery site in 1865. The two buildings illustrated (Numbers UB1 and UB2) remain standing to the present day (see Figures 24–26). Most of the kiln was demolished in 1896 (Figure 19).

As this view illustrates, the quayside area was extended out onto the River Lagan in the years following the pottery's closure. When the pottery was working, the Lagan shore would have adjoined the quayside building (Building 1).

The earliest available map of the site (1815) clearly indicates that the pottery possessed only one free-standing kiln by that date, set within the central courtyard of the pottery (Figure 15, p 15).[106] From the excavation, we now know that the internal diameter of the oven was 15 feet, while the outer hovel was 36 feet in diameter (suggesting a considerable height of around 55–65 feet). But even though these dimensions are slightly larger than is usual, the kiln still seems comparatively small for a pottery of this size. (The early Belleek pottery had two kilns, by comparison.) There could be three very different reasons for this: either Greg was unable to complete a full complement of kilns before he died in 1796; perhaps other kilns were built, but were demolished before the 1815 map was surveyed; or possibly the remaining kilns, rather than being free-standing, were incorporated within the surrounding pottery buildings (and hence do not stand out on the 1815 map). There must, at least, have been a small enamelling kiln that the map does not show.

Another building excavated (Building EB1, Figure 15, p 15), is more anonymous, as no part of this building remains above ground, but it helps to place a date on the pottery deposits that were found. The fact that this building's foundations cut through the extensive layer of kiln waste that occurs all over the site suggests that it was built after the pottery had commenced operation. From documentary evidence we know that building work ceased in 1793, so that the pottery layer must date from c.1790–93. This is unfortunate in some respects,

Figure 23. A present-day view of the quayside wall that was built along the Lagan shore of the Downshire Pottery and Victor Coates' pottery. The entire structure, like the Downshire Pottery, was built of finely-dressed red sandstone from Scrabo Hill, near Newtownards, County Down. The lower portion of the wall is original, while the more haphazard upper section is 19th century in date, constructed from sandstone blocks that were presumably scavenged from pottery buildings which no longer remain.

because it means we have no clues as to what might have been produced after 1800 when the pottery was revived. Presumably the kiln waste from this later period was dumped farther out, away from the working area, on a part of the site that has not yet been found.

Even with the evidence of all of these buildings, however, both standing and buried, it is difficult to estimate the original size of the Downshire Pottery and its workforce. Perhaps the best estimate at this stage can be derived from the only comparable pottery building in Ireland; the main portion of the Belleek Porcelain Works (completed in 1866), which at 160 feet long by 33 feet wide and 56 feet high actually appears to have been slightly smaller than the main Downshire building.[107] Belleek employed 180 persons in 1869, even though the pottery site (1.4 acres) was also smaller than that of the Downshire Pottery (c.3.0 acres).[108]

For the present, because of the industrial nature of the site on which the buildings are situated, it is impossible to carry out a definitive survey. Until this has been done, estimates of the pottery's size must obviously remain speculative, but the present 'best-guess' of those who have been most closely involved in examining the site is that the Downshire Pottery was probably built to accommodate a workforce in the region of 200–300 persons. Viewing the enterprise as a whole, it even seems possible that Thomas Greg may actually have modelled the Downshire Pottery on one of Wedgwood's most successful rivals – the Leeds (creamware) Pottery. It must be stated, however, that unlike Leeds, the Downshire Pottery probably never realised its full potential. Certainly the value of its annual output appears only to have been a fraction of that of its English counterpart.

Figure 24. A present-day view of the best-preserved of the remaining Downshire Pottery buildings, (Building UB1). The original (sandstone) quayside of the pottery remains intact, two feet below the surface of the yard to the right. The tall conical kiln was situated to the left of this building.

Although barely visible today, the red, dressed Scrabo sandstone river-wall, with the tall, red sandstone pottery behind, must once have been a large and handsome group of buildings. To the inhabitants of Belfast, who had an uninterrupted view across the river Lagan of both the Downshire pottery and the new glasshouses, these ambitious ventures on the far riverbank must have represented a dramatic indicator of the town's commercial fortunes, as they waxed and waned during the troubled years of the late 18th century.

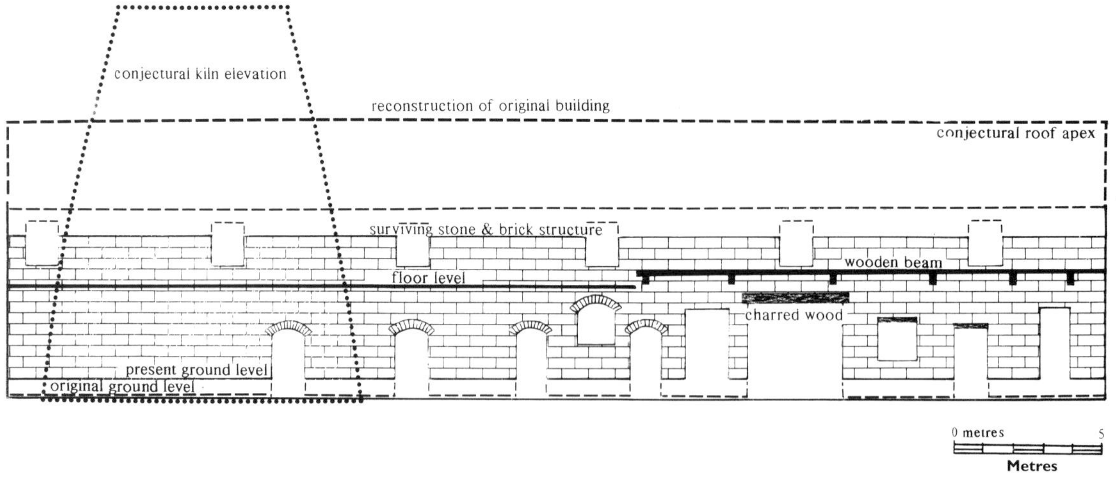

Figure 25. A schematic drawing of Building UB1. The top of the building was lost in a fire c.1900. The interior floor level, like most of the site, has been raised c.2–3 feet in height since the time the pottery was working. Today this gives the impression that the doors and archways are unusually low.

Figure 26. The south facing side of the second original Downshire Pottery building (Building UB2). The original, large window arches can still be discerned even though the building has subsequently undergone at least five major phases of alteration. This was probably the location of the painting and decorating rooms (see Figure 27).

Figure 27. The painting and decorating room of an English 'Staffordshire-type' pottery, c.1840. Note the larger windows on the right-hand wall, similar to those that survive at the Downshire Pottery (Figure 26). From an early 19th-century English print, author's collection.

NOTES

1. PJ Francis, 'The early fine-ceramic potteries of Belfast and the Carrickfergus clay trade', unpublished MA thesis, the Queen's University of Belfast, 1992.
2. See acknowledgements for a full list of sponsors of the Belfast Potteries Project.
3. Readers seeking further details will find them in PJ Francis, 'The Belfast Potthouse, Carrickfergus clay and the spread of the delftware industry', in *English Ceramic Circle Transactions*, 15, pt 2 (1994), pp 271–99. See also Francis (2000), Chapter 1, *'The Belfast Posthouse'.*
4. MSD Westropp, 'Notes on the pottery manufacture in Ireland', in *Proceedings of the Royal Irish Academy*, 32, sect C, no. 1 (1913); *Irish pottery and porcelain*, General Guide to the Art Collections, National Museum of Ireland (1935). M Archer, *Irish delftware*, ROSC exhibition catalogue, Castletown House, County Kildare, Dublin (1971).
5. M Dunlevy (as M Reynolds), 'Irish fine-ceramic potteries, 1769–96', *Post-Mediaeval Archaeology*, 18 (1984), pp 251–61.
6. Ibid, p 251.
7. Ibid.
8. Ibid, pp 251–2.
9. Ibid, p 251. The applications were made for the periods March 1772–73 and March 1773–74.
10. Ibid, p 252. Advertisement from Saunder's *News Letter*, 11–14 June 1773, p 1.
11. Ibid, p 252. Stacey & Co failed to claim the premium offered for April 1774 to March 1775.
12. R Hampson, 'Longton Potters 1700–1865', in *Journal of Ceramic History*, 14 (1990), pp 145–6.
13. Dunlevy, 'Irish fine-ceramic potteries', pp 252–3.
14. Ibid, p 253. John Angel's *General History of Ireland In Its Ancient and Modern State* (1781), is especially inaccurate in respect of the delftware pottery at Rostrevor (treating 37-year-old information as 'current'). The Wedgwood reference is given at note 22, p 153.
15. Hampson, 'Longton Potters', pp 46–8. The Chetham surname features in Longport from 1796, although an Edward Chetham does not appear to be recorded.
16. Dunlevy, 'Irish fine-ceramic potteries', p 253. The *Dublin Chronicle* article appeared 6–8 September 1787.
17. G Benn, *A History of the Town of Belfast*, vol. 1 (London, 1877), p 300. The rapidly growing population of Belfast was 13,105 in 1782 and 18,320 in 1791. The population of Dublin is taken from Walker's *Hibernian* magazine (December 1788), pp 666–7.
18. P Walton, *Creamware and other English Pottery at Temple Newsham House, Leeds* (Bradford and London, 1976), p 77.
19. Dunlevy, 'Irish fine-ceramic potteries', pp 252, 255–9. See also M Dunlevy (Reynolds), 'Wedgwood in Dublin, 1772–77', in *Irish Arts Review*, 1, no. 2 (1982), pp 8–14.
20. *Report of a house of lords committee* (1785), reference at note 22. Testimony of John Blades, cut glass manufacturer, p 6. Corroborated by MSD Westropp, *Irish glass* (1920), various pages.
21. J Kelly, *Prelude to Union: Anglo-Irish politics in the 1780s* (Cork, 1992), pp 114–16.
22. The Staffordshire potters' petition was submitted 6 April 1785. See *Journal of the House of Commons*, 40 (1784–85), p 781. Wedgwood's testimony in June 1785 is recorded in: 'Minutes of the evidence taken before a committee of the house of lords... appointed to take into consideration the resolutions come to by the commons, relative to the adjustment of the commercial intercourse between Great Britain and Ireland', *House of Lords Sessional Papers* (1785), pp 144–66.
23. Ibid, pp 145, 153–4, 156–7.
24. Ibid, p 147.
25. The only commercial-scale earthenware manufacturer using white-firing Irish clays today is Nicholas Mosse at Kilkenny, who tolerates a higher than usual wastage-rate in order to use these local clays. Good quality ball-clays were produced from an open pit at Coalisland in County Tyrone until 1995, and recent firing-test analysis suggests that these specific clays were used by the Downshire Potters to produce their 'buff-bodied wares'. (See also note 53.)
26. Referenced in Kelly, *Prelude to Union*, p 153. The quotation is from the *Dublin Evening Post*, 10 May 1785, and is attributed to Lecky by S Millin, *Sidelights on Belfast history* (Belfast, 1932), p 65.
27. *BNL* 5–9 August 1785, p 3. Greg was co-signatory of an appeal by the Belfast chamber of commerce, urging 'the inhabitants of Belfast' in the strongest terms to reject the commercial resolutions.
28. Kelly, *Prelude to Union*, pp 208–9 *et seq.* Hopes for reform remained high until 1787 at least, when a new Navigation Act was passed, but dwindled slowly thereafter. The main economic decline did not occur until c.1796.
29. For reference to 'similar fabric to that of Wedgwood' see note 57.
30. RWM Strain, *Belfast and its charitable society* (London, 1961), pp 80–1, and S Millin, *Sidelights on Belfast history*, pp 134–5.
31. J Smyth, *Belfast Directory for 1807* (Belfast, 1807). John Ashmore's general-merchants premises in Belfast were at 54 Waring Street, Stephenson's surgery was at number 70.
    Ashmore's advertisements suggest that he was principally a dealer in barilla, a soda ash employed in glass manufacture which may also have been of value to the pottery (eg *BNL* 29 July 1791).
    This individual may have been the John Ashmore who died in Belfast in September 1827, aged 61, in which case he was only 21 years of age when the pottery was established. See ACW Merrick and RSJ Clarke, *Old Belfast families and the new burying ground* (Belfast, 1991), p 12.
32. MB Rose, *The Gregs of Quarry Bank Mill* (Cambridge, 1986), pp 1–4, 13–15 and 140. See also DJ Sidebotham, *Catalogue of the Greg Collection of English Pottery*, Manchester City Art Gallery (1923); M Parkinson, 'The Thomas Greg collection of English pottery', in

English Ceramic Circle Transactions, 8, Pt 1 (1971), p 42. The Thomas Tylston Greg (1858–1920) who formed this collection of English pottery was great-great grandson of the Thomas in Belfast.

33. Ibid, pp 13–15. NE Gamble, 'The business community and trade in Belfast 1767–1800', unpublished doctoral dissertation, University of Dublin, 1978, various pages. See also G Chambers, *Faces of change: the Belfast and Northern Ireland Chambers of Commerce and Industry 1783–1983* (Belfast, 1984), pp 69–72.
34. G Benn, *A history of the town of Belfast*, vol 2 (London, 1880), p 182. When the pottery was being set up in 1787, Greg was also in possession of a coal-exploration lease on Belfast's Cave Hill, just a few miles from the town. PRONI, Donegall Ms, D/509/653, Donegall to Thomas Greg, 11 January 1785.
35. Ibid, p 181.
36. For a thorough account of Cunningham, see Chambers, *Faces of change*, pp 35–48.
37. Strain, *Belfast and its charitable society*. Details of Stephenson's appointment are on p 81. Greg played a crucial role in running the lottery which funded the society's establishment in 1753–54, pp 18–24.
38. Ibid, pp 136–8 *et seq*.
39. See Appendix 1, paragraph 2 .
40. Westropp (1935), 'Notes on the pottery manufacture in Ireland', p 19. Delamain's advertisement is dated 17 September 1754.
41. PJ Francis, 'The early fine-ceramic potteries of Belfast', pp 110–34. The pottery assemblage was collected by the author in August 1992, subsequent to submittal of this thesis. It includes several misfired fragments of cobalt-painted delftware and c.20 fragments of delftware biscuit, one of which is the base of a vase or drug jar.
42. Ulster Museum Acc. No. 37–1918. The author is indebted to Mr R Heslip, Curator, History Department, for his help in finding this tile and for his remarks on local brass examples; and to Michael Archer of the Victoria and Albert Museum, for the comments which appear in the photograph caption. The James Reilly to whom the tile belonged was a well-known character in Carrickfergus, 'one of the eccentric figures of the Evangelical Revival' who later moved to Southwark. See N Curnock (ed), *The Journal of the Rev John Wesley, AM* (London, 1909), vol IV, pp 178–9.
43. The initial spur to Ballymacarret's development was in 1779, when the area was purchased by the Irish Patriot MP the Rt Hon Baron Barry Yelverton. The first industry to set up was the flint-glasshouse of Benjamin Edwards, which opened in 1781. (*BNL* 9–12 January 1781, p 3). The rapid growth of Ballymacarret led to a bizarre conflict with the Donegall family (the owners of Belfast), to whom Yelverton sold out in 1787. This new stability in the ownership of the 'Grand-Lease' may have influenced the setting up of Downshire Pottery in that same year. (Information courtesy T McErlean.)
44. The area marked on the 1791 map (see frontispiece) as 'Intended Improvements', surrounding the glasshouses, was reclaimed using quarry stones and glasshouse-waste. The 1993 excavations have shown that pottery-waste was extensively used as land-fill in the vicinity of the pottery also. See also notes 51 and 81.
45. WA McCutcheon, *The industrial archaeology of Northern Ireland*, Fairleigh Dickinson University Press (1984), p 58. A letter to the *Belfast News Letter* (*BNL* 8–11 February 1794, p 3), shows that Tyrone coals were used by Smylie's bottle glasshouse at that date, but essentially, these coal deposits proved extremely disappointing and brought financial ruin to many who were involved in them.
46. *BNL* 2 July 1784. 'Wanted for building a new Glass House, quarry stones &c...'.
47. *Statutes at large passed in the parliaments held in Ireland* (Dublin, 1786): years 23, 24 George III, Chap. 1, para. 31. (1783–84 Session, vol 12, p 41).
48. Reported as 'about 120' feet in height when opened (*BNL*, 19 August 1785), and as '150 feet high' when sold (*BNL*, 16 September 1823). The cone was demolished following storm damage on 11 October 1937, but the base was only removed (unrecorded) in 1981. See CRG McClure, *Artery of the east* (Belfast, c.1990), p 2.
49. *BNL*, 19 August 1785, p 3, indicates the cone was completed on Saturday 13 August.
50. S Millin, *Sidelights on Belfast history*, p 77. The partnership (with Greg as principal of 13 merchants) was registered 12 September 1785, then re-organised and re-registered with 12 partners on 22 September 1791. Their first advertisement is in *BNL* 21–25 April 1786, p 3. In consequence of the Anonymous Partnerships Act, Greg's senior partnership may not have been public knowledge during his lifetime.
51. *BNL* 16–19 May 1786, p 3. See also *BNL* 7–10 June 1791, p 3.
52. Belfast reference *BNL* 8–11 May 1787, p 2.
    Dublin reference Westropp, 'Notes on the pottery manufacture in Ireland', p 6. From the *Dublin Chronicle*, 15 May 1787.
53. The famed Carrickfergus delftware clays were wholly unsuitable for creamware manufacture. For further information see PJ Francis, 'The Belfast Potthouse, Carrickfergus clay and the spread of the delftware industry', in *English Ceramic Circle Transactions*, 15, Pt 2 (1994), p 271.
54. *BNL* 31 May 1792. Their wares are included at the end of this advertisement as 'N.B. The Cream Colour Ware of the Manufactory of Messrs. Gregg [sic], Stephenson and Ashmore, sold as above'.
55. Ms. map in the Linenhall Library, Belfast, dated 1789.
56. Even though the prominent free-standing kiln was not shown on this map, the widespread deposits of pottery waste found during the excavation suggest that the kiln was firing from a very early stage.
57. Coates' 'superior kind of black-glazed ware' is referred to in G Dubordieu, *A statistical survey of the county of Down* (Dublin, 1802), p 19. That Dubordieu was referring to Coates' pottery is shown by his statement that 'at the same place there is also a manufacture of starch', but Coates demolished both pottery and starchworks in 1798 to build an iron foundry. Despite the

publication date, therefore, Dubordieu's visit probably took place as early as c.1797–98.

58. The 1791 'enumeration' of Belfast was conducted by R Hyndman, but the original does not appear to have survived. It is referred to in DA Beaufort, *Memoir of a map of Ireland* (London, 1792), p 23.
59. J Carlyle, *Statistical account of Scotland* (Edinburgh, 1791). Information courtesy of G Haggarty, Edinburgh.
60. Dunlevy, 'Irish fine-ceramic potteries', p 254. The flint mill was complete by December 1795. (Proceedings of the Dublin Society, 17 December 1795, p 33.)
61. Proceedings of the Dublin Society, 22 March 1792, p 66.
62. See note 54.
63. *BNL* 12–15 June. 1792, p 3.
64. *BNL* 8–11 February 1794, p 3. The glass house was 'on a plan hitherto unknown and unattempted in this country'.
65. The petition to the Irish Parliament, January 1793 (Appendix, paragraph 5) states that 'several additional Buildings are necessary to the greater Extent and Perfection of it'.
66. Dunlevy, 'Irish fine-ceramic potteries', p 257. Details from Dublin Registry of Deeds, Book 460, p 37, no 293128, Greg and others to Johnston, 20 September 1792. Greg, Stephenson and Ashmore sold to Mary Johnson of Ballymacash and Ann Johnson of Lisburn, spinsters, a plot of land 60 feet broad at the road, extending back 100 feet 'or thereabouts' towards the river, with the full river rights. This plot may be one which is still held under a separate lease to the present day, on the northern edge of the pottery site.
67. *BNL* 9–13 November 1792, p 3.
68. Parliamentary support was provided through the Dublin Society. During Downshire's first year they were allowed to claim against manufactured goods up to £600 in value, but with parliamentary support this ceiling was raised to £2000. As Downshire only claimed for manufacture worth around £1000 per annum, they earned around £100 per annum in premiums (as opposed to the previous maximum of £60).
69. This is the earliest reference to the pottery as the 'Downshire Pottery', named thus by Greg himself. The name recurs in their Dublin Society applications, but most of their subsequent advertisements retain the previous 'Greg, Stephenson and Ashmore's pottery'. The marquess died in 1793, which may further explain why no such personalised dinner-service appears to have survived.
70. Petition to the Irish house of commons, 29 January 1793. PRONI T/533/5.
71. J Bardon, *A history of Ulster* (Belfast, 1992), p 221. Britain also entered the war with France in February 1793, heightening tensions between these garrisons and some potentially pro-French Belfast liberals.
72. *BNL* 22 April 1793. This advertisement ran until 15 June, then re-appeared for a further month on 27 September.
73. *Belfast Northern Star*, 25 November 1793. The same advertisement, without the manganese reference, appeared for one month in *BNL* from 29 November 1793.
74. Proceedings of the Dublin Society, 13 November 1794, pp 10–11.
75. *Belfast Northern Star*, 18–21 May 1795, p 1 (and following issues until 15–18 June). 'Greg, Stevenson[sic], & Ashmore Are selling cream-coloured and painted Earthenware, at their Pottery in Ballymacarret. A person attends for this purpose, from ten before noon, till three after noon. Dealers in this branch, will find it advantageous, if they apply soon'.
76. Proceedings of the Dublin Society, 28 April 1796, p 106. The lease of this mill also makes clear that the flint mill was Greg's alone, not the property of the pottery partnership.
77. Dunlevy, 'Irish fine-ceramic potteries', p 253. From Proceedings of the Dublin Society, 20 June 1793, 19 June 1794 and 28 April 1796.
78. *BNL* 8–11 January 1796, p 3. *Belfast Northern Star* 7–11 January 1796, p 3.
79. Dunlevy, 'Irish fine-ceramic potteries', p 254. From Dublin Registry of Deeds, Book 506, p 110, no 328171, relating to a lease dated 20 August 1796. Cunningham Greg sold the 'Flint Mill, with the Machinery, Dams, Weirs and Watercourses' at Edenderry near Belfast, to William, John and Joseph Stevenson and John Holmes Houston for £455 (with some adjoining land).
80. See note 57.
81. *BNL* 30 June–4 July 1794, p 3. Notice of auction sale on 14 July 1794 of 870 feet by 370 feet. of reclaimed land 'adjoining the Glass-House'.
82. *BNL* 24–28 April 1797, p 3. The glasshouse sold off its draft horses and carts, blacksmith's equipment, coals and a large number of empty barrels. Excise duties on bottle glass, equivalent to those which prevailed in England, came into effect from 1 May 1797 (37, George III, chapter 28). Although it was intended that Smylie's large glasshouse should primarily produce window glass, bottles were probably its mainstay.
83. Westropp, *Irish glass*, London (1920) p 109, states that John Smylie & Co appears in Dublin trade directories from 1800–20, even though Smylie was by then a police commissioner and had ceased to be a partner in 1799 (see note 84). Repeated attempts by Cunningham Greg and heirs to sell the glasshouse between 1809 and 1823 were unsuccessful.
84. Memorial of an Indented Deed of Release, 2 February 1799, presently in possession of Sir Charles Brett Esq, Belfast. Cunningham Greg contracted to the absolute purchase by paying £223 to the seven other surviving partners.
85. *BNL* 29 October 1799, p 3.
86. LM Cullen, *An economic history of Ireland since 1660*, 2nd edn (London, 1987), p 100. Belfast was placed under martial law on 13 March 1797 and remained so until after the emergency. From H Joy, *Historical collections relative to the town of Belfast* (Belfast, 1817), p 461 *et seq.*
87. *BNL* 16 December 1800, p 3.
88. Most tradesmen visiting Belfast to sell from warehouses seem to have stated their place of origin ('just arrived from London', Dublin, etc). From various personal communications, (P Half-penny, G Haggarty, H Kelly), the Tennant or

Tennent name does not appear to be a known potter's surname either in Staffordshire, or in east or west Scotland, nor does it seem to be recorded in published sources. See Chambers, *Faces of change* for further details concerning Tennent.

89. Benn, *A history of the town of Belfast*, vol 2, p 23. These comments are handwritten beside the Tennent's pottery reference in FJ Bigger's personal copy of this book (Dublin private collection).
90. ATQ Stewart *pers. comm.* Several references preserved in the correspondence of Major General Nugent, the commanding officer in Belfast in 1798, indicate that Cunningham Greg was suspected of being in sympathy with the United Irishmen's cause. He may even have played a role in one particularly famous incident concerning the hiding of a Volunteer cannon. The brass field piece, briefly fired in Antrim during the rebellion, avoided detection in 1798, but is now believed to have been hidden in large air ducts that lay below the furnaces of Smylie & Co's glasshouse. Cunningham Greg was the principal owner of Smylie & Co's glasshouse at this time.
91. Holden's *Triennial Directory*, 4th edn for 1805–8 (London, 1805), vol 2, *Belfast Directory*, p 1. As the pottery was in Ballymacarret (County Down), not in Belfast (County Antrim), it is not listed individually.
92. Smyth, *Belfast Directory for 1807*.
93. HE Kelly, 'The career of James Stevenson in Greenock', in *Journal of the Northern Ceramic Society*, 11 (1994), pp 35–46. Stevenson is first recorded in Greenock in 1809, as a china and stoneware merchant. See also V Boa, PC Denholm and GF Quail, *The Clyde Pottery Greenock* (Greenock, 1987).
94. See note 79.
95. For glass reference see note 84. Stevenson's ownership of Mount Pottinger, 'Mr. Cunningham's' and 24 acres of ground is recorded in PRONI, D/509/830: Stevenson to Cunningham, 20 September 1792. Millin, *Sidelights on Belfast history*, p 68, indicates that a petition supporting the Act of Union was signed by James, John and Robert Stevenson, and a James Stevenson junior. The 1819 *Belfast Trade Directory* also lists a James Stevenson as a copper-plate engraver.
96. RM Young, 'The old Belfast china manufactory at Ballymacarret', in *Ulster Journal of Archaeology*, 2, pt 3 (1896), pp 188–9.
97. Westropp, 'Pottery manufacture in Ireland', plate III.
98. For help in this initial excavation, the author would like to record his sincere gratitude to Professor Mike Baillie, Felicity Graham, Rosie Agar, Emily Bennett, Raymond Bennett, Jane Castles, Valerie Cooper, Mandy Crawford, Charles Dickinson, Mavis Dickinson, Rosemary Henry, Peter Meanley, Janey Sproule and Roberta Rea.
99. This material was amalgamated with the larger assemblage of pottery fragments recovered later. However, as this deposit was comparatively rich in decorated wares, many of these shards recovered from the initial 'rescue' excavation are now stored with the principal 'Downshire' collection in the Ulster Museum, (rather than mixed with bulk, biscuit-ware samples kept in the Museum's secondary stores.
100. Two-thirds of the kiln remain under a previously-built concrete laneway. As a result of the site-owners' co-operation, the one-third which was excavated was subsequently built over in a non-destructive fashion, by constructing a decorative brick 'waterfall' feature. A layer of sand approximately one foot thick was laid on top of the excavated kiln surface to facilitate easier re-excavation, should the need arise, at some future date.
101. The excavation was conducted by the author, Tom McErlean, Andy Dickson, Laura Francis, Melanie Reid, Vaughn Gibson, Nick Lewis and Roseanne Meenan.
102. S Lewis, *A topographical dictionary of Ireland* (London, 1837), vol 1, p 143. Now that independent evidence exists to corroborate their assertions, many of the grand-seeming statements in Greg, Stephenson and Ashmore's Petition to the Irish Parliament (appendix, p 00) also appear simply to state the truth.
103. 'A bird's eye view of Belfast in 1865', reprinted by the Linen Hall Library (Belfast, 1985).
104. Twenty feet of the original 150 feet length was removed c.1985, and the tops of the walls were lost through fire c.1900, but basically the building is in good, restorable condition. The original floor is also probably preserved, two to three feet below the present ground level.
105. Trenches 8 and 9 encountered only post-c.1807 landfill. The site contractor's pipe-laying trenches in this area have occasionally come across the sandstone quayside at a depth of around three feet.
106. The 1815 map of Belfast, published by Marcus Ward & Co, is extremely inaccurate, but agrees with more accurate 1819 and 1823 revisions which also show only one kiln.
107. JB Cunningham, *The story of Belleek* (Belleek, 1992), p 22.
108. Ibid, p 25. Areas were based on the 1872 Ordnance Survey sheet for Belleek and the 1823 Marcus Ward map of Belfast.

Abbreviations

BNL	*Belfast News-Letter*
PRO (NI)	Public Record Office of Northern Ireland
PRO (Kew)	Public Record Office, Kew, London

The Wares

Introduction

Having looked at the history of the pottery, and having explored the site, one very substantial question remains, namely, what did the Downshire Pottery's 'Irish creamware' actually look like?

One of the main reasons that the Downshire Pottery has been largely forgotten is that its potters employed no distinguishing factory mark of any kind. We can be reasonably certain that this was the case, because during the last century, ever since collectors first began looking for Irish creamware, not a single marked piece has turned up. At one stage in this research it was believed that a rare, impressed 'crown' mark had indeed been identified, but it now appears that this is probably an English mark.[1]

Researchers elsewhere, studying similarly anonymous potteries, have found that attributions can sometimes come from 'documentary pieces'; examples of pottery which, because of an unusual inscription or a known provenance, can be attributed to one specific source. Alas, if the Downshire Pottery did make special presentation pieces for notable Irish worthies of the time, then their descendants have not remembered the gesture. We may wonder whether the pieces of Downshire creamware which Thomas Greg contemplated making for the Marquess of Downshire in 1793 still survive, or indeed, whether they were ever made, (p 9). But even if they do, the fact that not one documentary example of Downshire pottery has been located in the last century means it is unlikely that such pieces will lead to new attributions at this late stage.

In their absence, and without the benefit of even a few marked pieces, the only alternative we are left with is to use the pottery fragments that were excavated from the site itself as a starting point for attributions. It was for this reason that such pains were taken to collect, prepare and catalogue the material that was recovered, even though, by English standards, the total assemblage is small. Given that the working life of the Downshire Pottery was short, surviving examples will also be rare for that reason. Even so, the intact pieces illustrated in this book have all turned up in local antique shops and collections during the few years since the excavation, which suggests that other examples still exist and await discovery.

Preparation and Sorting

With the exception of one small part of the assemblage, the enormous amount of washing, sorting and cataloguing which the excavated material required was all carried out by one person, Linda Canning. The work took an entire year and – at the outset especially – represented a formidable task. Reading through this catalogue now, Linda's work might appear straightforward – it is difficult to realise that the pottery did not come out of the ground neatly grouped into recognisable objects in alphabetical order. Instead, it consisted of thousands of pieces of iron-stained and dirty, plain white pottery, mixed with mud, clinker and kiln furniture. The fact that we can now gain so much information from the assemblage is entirely the result of Linda's genuinely exceptional efforts.

To understand how the assemblage or 'collection' has been sorted and catalogued we need to look briefly at the excavation and post-excavation work that was carried out. As described earlier (see 'The excavations', p 14), there were two different investigations of the site, which together produced the pottery fragments that now make up this single assemblage; an initial 'rescue' excavation and a subsequent 'formal' excavation, (particularly the material from Trench 4). On both occasions, and during the formal excavation especially, efforts were made to collect and bag material from each individual square metre as it was excavated. This was done in the hope that, after the finds had been washed and sorted, it would then be easier to reconstruct pieces that had been broken *in situ*. Unfortunately, it transpired that the pottery had been so mixed up and jumbled *before* burial that even with careful collection it was only rarely possible to reconstruct full shapes. The fact that the pottery shards were so mixed suggests that they had not originally been taken straight from the kiln and dumped onto the ground nearby; rather, they were probably first shovelled into wheelbarrows and taken to larger stockpiles, then taken later to the part of the site where they were finally scattered. At each stage, the shards would have become more mixed and broken up, which in turn made reconstruction of the pottery extremely difficult. We shall never know if this is precisely how the material was originally deposited, but the interpretation would certainly explain why so few full profiles of the pottery vessels were found, despite our best efforts over several months.

1. The crown mark was described in both the *English Ceramic Circle Transactions*, 15, pt 2 (1994), and the *Irish Arts Review Yearbook* (1997). This mark is now attributed to Neale and Co, (English creamware manufacturers working at the same time as the Downshire Pottery).

When it eventually became evident that attempting to 'reconstruct' pots was not likely to be successful, a different, less ambitious strategy was adopted. All of the excavated shards were examined to determine just how many different types of object were present (jugs, bowls, teapots, etc), and then the most complete example of each was lifted out and retained separately in a group which later became the 'type collection'. (This included material from both the rescue and the formal excavations.) All of the most useful, decorated wares were similarly retained with this 'type collection', as were representative examples of the different varieties of 'diagnostic feature' (handles, lids, spouts, etc) and kiln furniture.

The assemblage of excavated Downshire pottery, illustrated and described here, and now in the Ulster Museum, is therefore stored as two 'collections':

1. The *'type' collection*, which contains the best examples recorded of all of the different forms, together with all of the decorated fragments (approximately 20 kilograms of material in total).

2. The *'bulk' collection*, retained in bags in storage and not readily accessible, which consists of all of the other shards recovered from both the rescue and the formal excavations. These are all bagged according to the square metre of the excavation from which they originally came (approximately 100 kilograms of material in total).

Some Cautionary Remarks

The most important point to be borne in mind is that the Downshire pottery assemblage is much smaller than most of those which have appeared in print previously (the assemblages recorded in England at Greatbatch's Pottery and Bovey Tracey, for example, were much larger). This small sample size gives rise to two evident forms of bias in the assemblage;

1. About 60 per cent of the decorated shards were recovered from a small area of about three square metres. It is obvious therefore that the decorated wares are not representative of a wide range of Downshire Pottery wares – most seem to have come from a *single firing* of the pottery's kiln.

2. The white, biscuit-ware fragments appear to have been deposited very early in the pottery's history, having been employed to provide a working surface for the muddy pottery site, rather in the fashion of gravel or 'hard-core'. They are thus not representative of the entire duration of the pottery's working life. Rather, they date from the very early years of initial production. They provide few indications of the wares produced after c.1793.

As a result of this restricted range, evidence of sample bias can frequently be seen among the individual types of object recorded. For example, not one teacup was found, even though it is impossible to believe that a pottery of this size did not make teacups. Similarly, six different styles of plate were recorded, indicating that at least six different styles of dinner-set were manufactured, but (as Table 3.2 shows, p 57) only about 40 per cent of this range was actually recorded among the excavated shards.

The sample bias can, to a small extent, be compensated by the catalogue – Table 3.2 for example, is as useful for indicating the wares that could or *should* be there as for recording those that *were* found. More unfortunate perhaps is the small size of the assemblage, which means that some of the most interesting examples of Downshire wares are represented, tantalisingly, by just a few fragments. For example:

- there is only one shard of the most complex, moulded, 'Prattware'-style jug
- there are only two fragments of a complex, 'double-entwined' handle
- there are only three examples of moulded floral sprigs
- only four shards exhibit overglaze enamel decoration
- only one shard exhibits green-edged, marbled decoration
- no examples were found with any trace of printed decoration, despite the enigmatic pencil-written reference on one biscuit-ware shard to an order for '2 Printed' pots (Figure 25xii).

Considering that we must rely on such very small samples, it is extremely fortunate that virtually no 'contamination' appears to have been brought onto the Downshire Pottery site. Two fragments of a Liverpool porcelain tea bowl were the only obvious contemporary 'foreigners' noted, although there was widespread contamination of later deposits with a wide range of Victorian material.

A future investigation of the site would be most efficient if it was planned to take some of the factors discovered by this excavation into account. For example, we now know that a large and extensive layer of white biscuit-ware extends all over the site, but much of this material has been found to be of comparatively limited value in research terms, largely because it was badly broken up and mixed before burial. It would be much better in future to look for the occasional small pockets of glazed, *decorated* wares that turn up by chance, (as on the rescue excavation); in other words, a much smaller, opportunistic excavation might actually prove more successful than a major one which investigates the entire site methodically, and would require much less post-excavation work. There is no doubt that further decorated wares must yet be found for us to gain a true impression of the range of wares that the Downshire Pottery made, and of the general level of competence that was achieved.

Catalogue of Excavated Wares

THE excavated pottery fragments, and hence this catalogue, fall naturally into two main categories:

1. Glazed, decorated wares (coloured fragments).
2. Unglazed wares (plain white fragments).

For the purposes of identifying potential examples of Downshire Pottery, the first group – the decorated, glazed shards – are the most useful. Unfortunately, they are also by far the rarest of the two categories, representing just a few kilograms out of the hundreds of kilograms of material that was excavated.

As the coffee-pot that is attributed with certainty to Belfast demonstrates, however, (colour plates 11 and 20) just one of these coloured, decorated shards can be sufficient for establishing an attribution. For this reason, particular emphasis has been placed in this catalogue upon illustrating as many of these distinctive shards as possible *in colour*. Together with intact examples of Belfast creamware that have already been attributed as a result of the excavations, these coloured shards constitute Part 1 of this catalogue, (which centres on the colour photographs).

The unglazed biscuit-ware fragments that are described in Part 2 of the catalogue, on the other hand, are relatively uninformative by comparison – despite the fact that they were recovered in much larger quantity (approximately 100–150 kilograms). They have been classified according to object – the best example of all of the different forms recorded was retained in the 'Type Collection', even if the only fragment appeared small or unremarkable (eg, the basket fragments Figure 1i). This second group is principally illustrated in black and white. In some cases, where unusual mouldings were employed, (eg, the sauce-boat illustrated in 14, iii), the shapes alone may be sufficiently distinctive to allow attribution. More commonly, however, the forms recorded appear to be very similar to the products of creamware potteries elsewhere and so, without the additional clues provided by decoration, it is unlikely that these fragments will lead to new attributions on their own. Even so, establishing the range of vessels that were produced in Belfast is a valuable exercise, if only to gauge the potters' proficiency.

POTTERY TYPES

Four types of lead-glazed earthenware were recorded in total, each of which is illustrated in colour plate 1.

1. *Creamware* – (white-bodied).
2. *Pearlware* – (white-bodied).
3. '*Drab*' or *buff-bodied ware*.
4. Fine and coarse '*speckled*' *buff-bodied ware*.

Most abundant was creamware biscuit – which could have been intended for making either creamware or pearlware. (Pearlware and creamware bear an identical lead glaze, except that pearlware glaze has been tinted slightly with cobalt to a light blue colour.) Documentary evidence suggests that this white, creamware-biscuit was almost certainly produced using Irish white-firing clays, but not unexpectedly, there is no difference in visual appearance between these and English creamwares. (If there had been, then Irish creamware would have been recognised a long time ago.) The source of these clays has not yet been specifically identified, but firing tests and chemical analyses are presently being conducted on clay samples from Counties Antrim, Londonderry and Tyrone.

A very distinctive characteristic of some of the Downshire Pottery's creamwares – such as the coffee-pot shown in colour plate 20 – is that they have been grossly over-fired, and in the hand feel quite unlike comparable English creamwares. The creamware body of these over-fired examples is highly unusual and distinctive, having the appearance of a hybrid creamware/white stoneware, with obvious 'orange-peel' dimpling of the very thin, partly volatilised lead glaze. (When encountered on other excavations around Belfast in the past, such wares were generally mis-identified as 'Staffordshire white saltglaze'.) It is possible that the Downshire Pottery's advertisement in November 1792, which states that their creamware was now 'much superior to what it was', may suggest that this obvious problem with over-firing was solved at about that time.

Another firing defect that was found in abundance among the excavated shards was that the glaze often bore badly blemished 'patches', caused by a profusion of small, honey-coloured specks of iron contamination (Figure 28). Such blemishes can also be noted on some of the intact pieces that have been attributed to the Downshire Pottery (eg, the two platters shown in Catalogue section 13, 13 vi), but it is not clear as yet just how diagnostic of 'Belfast' this feature may be – it is quite possibly a widespread characteristic among English creamwares also.

The more utilitarian forms recorded, such as mugs and chamber pots, were often produced in a drab coloured 'buff-bodied' ware, the body deliberately speckled throughout with a peppering of minute dark inclusions (Pottery Types 3 and 4). Although similar buff-bodied wares were produced in England, intact

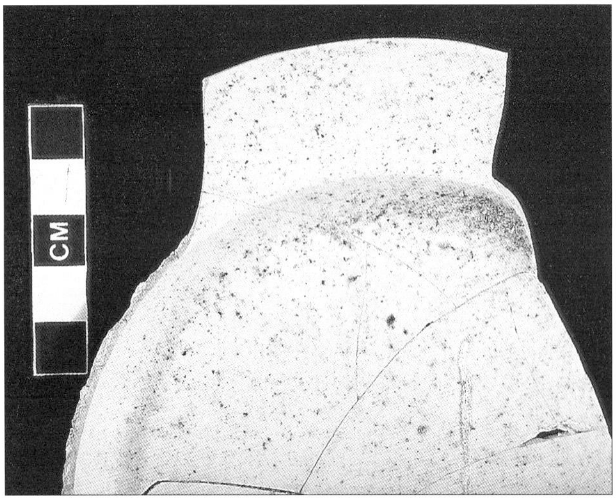

Figure 28. 'Peppered' iron spots on a glazed creamware waster.

examples are rare survivors, presumably because these vessels were utilitarian in character rather than decorative, and hence were not kept in the china cabinet. Firing tests have confirmed that the clays used for these buff-bodied wares came from Coalisland in County Tyrone (probably brought on the Lagan Canal to Belfast). The Downshire Pottery's saggars were made of the same buff-coloured clay, which had been tempered with a coarse sand and gravel 'grog'.

CATALOGUE, PART 1

COLOURED FRAGMENTS (COLOUR PLATES 2–12)

In view of the small quantity of coloured fragments found, no attempt has been made to group them into different categories of ceramic object, as has been done with the unglazed biscuit-wares described later. Instead, they have been sub-divided purely on the technique employed in their decoration. There are five basic groups, discussed in turn below;

1. Slip-decorated wares
   a. Plain slips
   b. Marbled slips
2. 'Tortoiseshell' or 'Whieldon-type' wares
3. Underglaze-painted wares
4. Painted shell-edged borders
5. Overglaze-enamelled wares

When minor variations in colour and secondary decoration are included, a total of 29 different decorative combinations can be recognised among the assemblage.

1. Slip-decorated wares

This is the simplest technique of decoration, achieved by dipping the pot into a suspension or 'slurry' of glaze colour, before dipping the pot for a second time in clear, lead-glaze. This produces a final piece of pottery which is of uniform colour overall, with a 'plain' or 'monochrome' slip (group 1a).

A more complex-looking but almost equally simple technique involves mixing several monochrome slips together. This produces wonderful, haphazard, mixed-colour designs; the group of wares generally known as 'marbled-slipwares', (group 1b).

***1a: Plain slipwares* (colour plates 2 and 13)**

All of the plain slipware fragments excavated were essentially brown in colour, varying in hue from a pure, dark brown (colour plate 2, top right) to a terracotta red-brown (colour plate 2, top left). They were recorded on a variety of objects, including jugs, sugar bowls and tankards.

Despite the relative simplicity of the technique, the monochrome wares were often finished to a high standard, usually enhanced with additional incised-line body decoration and borders. Two examples – a sugar bowl and tankard – bear finely-modelled floral sprigs as handle terminations (colour plate 2, top left and centre), suggesting they originally possessed delicate double-entwined or braided handles. In addition, one of the plain-slip decorated barrel jugs (colour plate 2, bottom right) exhibited an unusual style of 'combed' decoration, shown in more detail in Section 9D of the catalogue (see 9, vi, p 52).

On the basis of these finds, two large, baluster-shaped jugs have been attributed to the Downshire Pottery (colour plate 13). The first of these (left) is a large brown pearlware jug, 21 centimetres in height, formerly in the collection of the distinguished local dealer, Angus MacDonald, which matches precisely the colour of some of the excavated shards. This jug is also interesting in that the brown, monochrome slip was badly scratched *during* manufacture, indicating that the piece must originally have been sold as a second. Additional details of this jug are illustrated on page 75 and 78 (see 24, viii and 24, xx).

A second baluster jug, (colour plate 13, right), in a private collection in County Down, has also been attributed to the Downshire Pottery. Although blue-coloured monochrome-slipwares were not found on the excavation, the blue colour of this jug matches precisely the blue slip colour that was recorded among the Downshire Pottery's marbled-slipwares shards (see colour plate 8, centre right). In addition, the jug bears an overglaze, oil-painted decoration and the inscription 'Alderman Henderson, Hillsborough 1796', which enhances the Belfast attribution further. (Hillsborough, County Down, eight miles from Belfast, was the seat of the Marquess of Downshire).

Note also that both of these attributed jugs bear incised, engine-turned chequered bands around the body. Although such bands were not recorded among excavated shards, other types of engine-turned decoration were relatively common, and there is a very strong possibility that both jugs are Downshire products.

1b. Marbled slipwares **(colour plates 8 and 14)**
Three basic types of these very striking shards were found:

i. *Red-brown* (colour plate 8, top, left and bottom): invariably on a buff-coloured body. Mainly used as a decoration on utilitarian objects such as mugs, basins, chamber pots, etc. One very large jug fragment was also recorded (see Figure 9v, bottom shard).
ii. *Blue* (colour plate 8, centre): invariably used on a finer quality, creamware or pearlware body. Only jug body fragments were recorded.
iii. *Trailed-marble slip*, with green-edge (colour plate 8, top right). Only one rim shard was recorded, on a pale creamware body.

As on the monochrome slipwares, the top and bottom edges of these wares were usually finished off neatly with a simple, incised-line border.

At present, two locally purchased jugs are attributed to the Downshire Pottery on the basis of their similarity to these shards (colour plate 14). The first is a small (15 centimetre) baluster-shaped jug in a private collection in County Down (which also appears on the front cover).The colours of the buff-coloured body and red-brown marbling are identical to those observed in the red-brown shards above. In this case, however, the marbled decoration has been applied in such a way as to produce a distinctive and unusual feather or fan-shaped motif, repeated three times around the body.

The second jug (colour plate 14, right), in the author's collection, was also purchased locally. It compares precisely with the single, slip-trail decorated shard that was recovered from the Downshire site – even including the identical green-coloured rouletted border motif (colour plate 8, top right). Under normal circumstances this would be considered a very firm attribution to the Downshire Pottery, but because of the fact that only one such shard was recovered, the attribution must remain cautious as there is a chance that the shard may represent outside contamination. On the other hand, the broad barrel shape of this jug, and its complex border motif, seem to be more early 19th century in date than late 18th, in which case, it could well be that this jug actually represents an example of Downshire pottery that was produced during the later, revival period (1800–06), rather than during the initial phase of operation.

2. Tortoiseshell or 'Whieldon-type' decoration
(colour plates 3, 4, 9, 15 and front cover)
There are three variants of this style of decoration:

i. *Green 'splashed' decoration* (colour plate 3).
ii. *Brown 'sponged' or 'dabbed' decoration* (colour plate 4).
iii. *Brown and green mixed* (colour plate 9). All were recorded on creamware only (not on a buff-coloured body). This type of decoration is generally termed 'tortoiseshell' or 'Whieldon-type'.

A noticeable feature among this group of wares is that, in every case, the brown decoration has been applied by repeatedly dabbing the surface with a sponge or rag, whereas the green decoration, in every case, is simply 'splashed' or dripped onto the surface. These different styles of application remain true whether the green and brown colours were applied singly (colour plates 3 and 4) or together on one object (colour plate 9). The differences in the style of application are especially apparent on the tall, cylindrical mug that is attributed to the Downshire Pottery (see colour plate 16, right).

Despite the uniformity in technique, considerable variation was noted in the green and brown colours employed. The single-colour brown wares especially appear to have been produced using two different types of glaze pigment; iron and manganese, which resulted in colour gradation from true brown (iron, colour plate 4, bottom) to purple brown (manganese, colour plate 4, top).

All of these different colour variations appear to have been employed in the decoration of fine-quality wares, including teapots, coffee-pots, beakers and tankards, as well as all manner of dinner-wares and tureens.

Unfortunately, because such tortoiseshell-decorated wares were a standard product of many English creamware potteries, identifying an Irish example is extremely difficult. Only two pieces are presently attributed tentatively to the Downshire Pottery. The first is the tall cylindrical tankard mentioned previously (colour plate 16, right), which features a green colour of unusual hue that is also present among the excavated shards. The second is a round-bodied teapot (colour plate 15, left). This teapot bears two additional colours – yellow and blue – which were not recorded among the excavated shards, but the 'acanthus-moulded' spout provides a reasonable basis for the attribution nonetheless. Similar acanthus-moulded spouts were recorded in unglazed biscuit – see Figures 24iv, 24v. Both of these attributed examples came from the Angus Macdonald collection; the teapot was purchased originally in Ballyclare, County Antrim in 1952, the tankard in Belfast in 1966.

3. Underglaze-painted wares (colour plates 5, 10, 11, 12, 16, 20, 21 and 22)
The painted wares have been subdivided into three basic groups:

i. *Underglaze blue painted pearlwares*;
ii. *Yellow, green and brown painted creamwares*;
iii. *Other colour combinations.*

Figure 29. Border motif, cobalt blue on pearlware.

Among the painted wares in general, a variety of border motifs and repeating body motifs were recorded. For ease of reference, these have been summarised graphically in table form (colour plate 12).

***3i. Underglaze-blue painted pearlwares* (colour plate 10)**

The range of pearlware painted designs was relatively restricted, consisting primarily of standard 'oriental-style' landscapes (colour plate 10, top right), floral motifs (top left) and stylised, repeating motifs (bottom right).

In many cases, such as the complex stylised border shown in Figure 29 which appears on an eight inch diameter bowl, the quality of painting is not high. In other cases, however, (eg, on the teapot fragment which appears on the top left corner of colour plate 10), the painting is extremely fluid and professional – suggesting that the pottery employed painters with a wide range of abilities.

Unfortunately, because the style of underglaze blue painting is not especially distinctive, no examples of pearlwares have yet been attributed to the Downshire Pottery. The closest example yet found is a small, barrel-shaped jug shown in Figure 9, viii, which remains a highly speculative attribution for reasons explained on p 52.

***3ii. Yellow, green and brown painted creamwares* (colour plate 11)**

This distinctive decorative style is without doubt one of the most recognisable of the Downshire Pottery's range. Although variations exist in the tone of the green and brown employed, the bright, canary yellow is reasonably constant and unusual. No examples of English wares have been noted with this particular combination of colours.

The distinctiveness of this colour combination has acted as the basis for several attributions. The first and firmest attribution to come about was the spoutless coffee-pot shown in colour plate 20. This particular piece is also distinctive in that it has been over-fired to a near stoneware, comparable to many excavated shards. It was purchased in Saintfield, County Down in 1989.

The painted plate shown in colour plate 22 is also obviously related to this group, even though the standard yellow, green and brown palette has been further enhanced with cobalt blue. Although no precise matches for this border were recorded among the shards, details of the flower painting match those present on both the coffee-pot (colour plate 20) and the pearlware leaf-painted teapot described above (colour plate 10, top left).

The most spectacular piece identified to date, however, is a large baluster-shaped ale-jug in the Ulster Museum's collection (front cover, top centre and colour plate 21). Although the tone of the yellow, green and brown colour combination is slightly different to that seen in the shards, closer examination reveals obvious affinities with several of the painted details – the manner in which foliage has been represented, for example. Perhaps the greatest enigma of this ale-jug is why it should have been painted on each side with views of two very unusual buildings? Most likely, the illustrations were copied from contemporary prints, but the source has not yet been identified.

***3iii. Other painted colour combinations* (colour plate 5)**

This small group is essentially identical in overall character to the yellow, green and brown painted group described above, except that other colour combinations were recorded (see colour plate 5). Perhaps the most unusual are the teapot fragments decorated in underglaze blue, yellow and manganese brown or purple (colour plate 5, centre left).

On the basis of these shards, one small, locally purchased sparrowbeak jug has been attributed to the Downshire Pottery (colour plate 20). Apart from the difference in colour, the similarities in painting style to the yellow coffee-pot are obvious.

4. Painted shell-edged borders (colour plate 7)

This group is not strictly distinct from the underglaze-painted wares described in Group 3, but the extent of the 'painted' decoration is so rudimentary that they have been catalogued separately. As colour plate 7 shows, by far the majority of recorded borders were green-edged. Most plates of this type that have survived have a blue-painted edge, which reinforces the fact that sample bias exists among the excavated wares. Almost certainly, the great majority of these green-edged wares were the product of a single kiln-firing.

Nothing in the character of these borders is unique or distinctive; new attributions will more likely be based on the moulded details, rather than the border colouring.

5. Overglaze-enamelled wares (Colour plate 6)

The very small size of the excavated assemblage is most clearly seen in the overglaze-enamelled shards, only four of which were recorded during the entire excavation (colour plate 6). As overglaze enamels were fired at much lower temperatures than the underglaze decoration described above, their range of colours is correspondingly more varied, (including red and black, for example). With only four shards, however, it is impossible to gain any clear impression of the general range and level of quality that was achieved.

Nonetheless, these few shards do provide the basis for one very firm attribution. This is the unusual overglaze-enamelled teapot in the Ulster Museum (colour plate 15, right, and front cover, centre) bearing on one side the religious inscription 'No Cross No Crown' and on the other the longer quotation 'My Grace is Suffitiant for the Annah prince', (which should probably read 'My Grace is Sufficient For Thee, Anna [or Hannah] Prince'). It would be interesting to know more about Anna or Hannah Prince, but a swift scan of Belfast trade directories does not record the surname. Some of the details of the flower painting are identical to those seen on one of the Downshire Pottery shards, while the 'acanthus-moulded' spout also appears to be identical to excavated examples.

The only recorded enamel painter at the Downshire

Pottery is one Thomas Davis Bayley, who in February 1793 was training apprentices but was abruptly recalled to army duty, (see p 9). Given the highly naive character of the enamelling on this teapot, we can only presume that it was decorated by one of the apprentices.

OTHER ATTRIBUTIONS (COLOUR PLATES 17, 18, 19 AND 21)

In the course of researching the Downshire Pottery, a number of interesting pieces with obvious Irish associations have been found, but as they appear to be early 19th century in date there is nothing among the excavated material to connect them with the Downshire Pottery directly. Nonetheless, they each appear to be linked to Belfast by circumstantial evidence, and it is therefore possible that some or all of them were made here.

The source of a number of these attributions is a group of plain white, creamware oval dishes, bearing no marks, but with a finely modelled, moulded border decoration of harps and shamrocks (see Figure 11, p 13). A total of four such dishes have now been found in the Belfast area in the last five years, which could suggest they were locally produced, especially as one of these has been overfired to a hybrid creamware/white stoneware, similar in appearance to the well-attributed coffee-pot (colour plate 20). Because this border is too stylistically complex to be late 18th century in date, it has been tentatively attributed to the Downshire Pottery *after* 1800.

A slightly smaller border of precisely this pattern occurs on a wonderful group of circular pearlware plates, each of which features a vibrantly painted bird or animal. At least four examples are known in Ireland of the zebra design (colour plate 18), whilst the first recorded stag design turned up as recently as 1995 (colour plate 19). More recently again, a 'pea-fowl' design was recorded in America (Figure 30). The high-temperature colours of these painted designs are unlike any that were recorded among the (pre-1794) assemblage that was excavated. However, the colours are very similar to those which appear among a group of small jugs, painted with shamrock-crowned harps (colour plate 17). Two of the three known examples of these jugs were purchased in the Belfast area, and a similar design is also recorded on Belfast decanters of the same period (Figure 12, p 13).

To summarise these attributions, there seem to be two possibilities: either this group of plates and the small jugs were made in Belfast, but after 1800, during a period in which both documentary and excavated evidence is thin; or this group of plates and jugs with Irish motifs were made specifically for the Irish market and imported from England or Scotland in the early 19th century. For some reason, a higher proportion of these objects appear to have surfaced in the Belfast area than elsewhere in Ireland.

Figure 30. Peafowl design on a plate recently sold in America, featuring the 'Harp & Shamrock' moulded border.

For the present, either scenario would fit the evidence, but perhaps the attribution will become more satisfactorily resolved as new examples are discovered. Photographs of these objects have been included in this catalogue in the hope that new evidence will come to light as a result.

Plate 1. Pottery types (left to right): coarse and fine buff-bodied ware, creamware and creamware biscuit, pearlware

Plate 2. Plain or monochrome slip decoration

Plate 3. Splashed green decoration

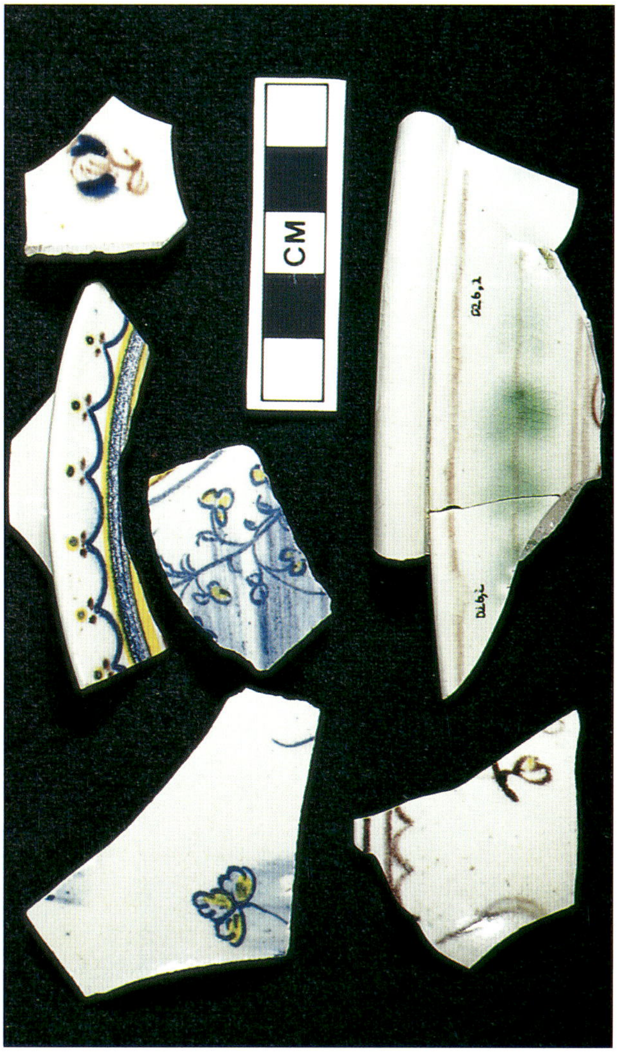

Plate 5. Unusual colour combinations

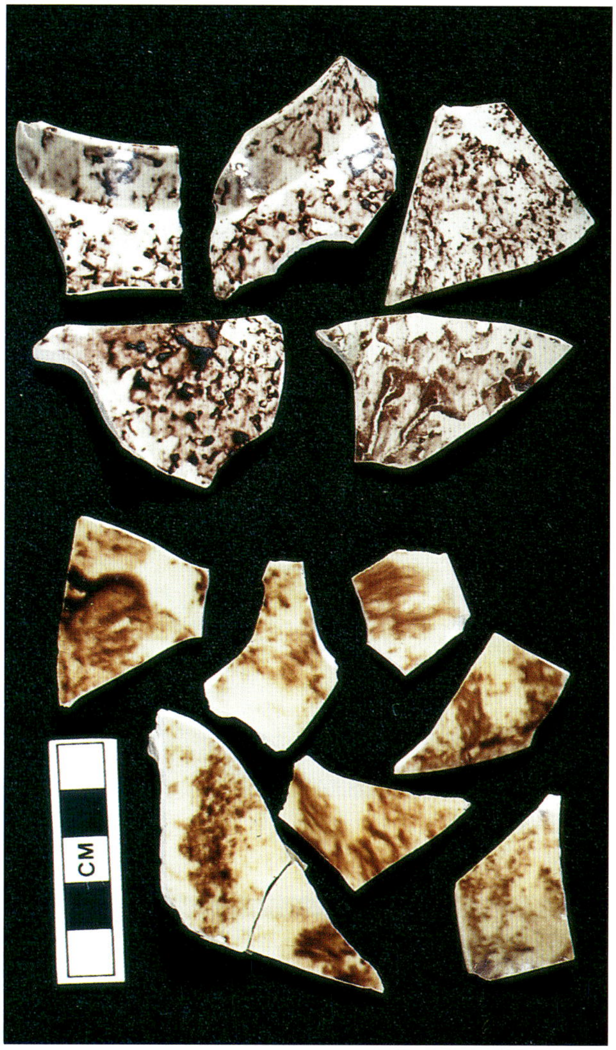

Plate 4. Dabbed brown decoration

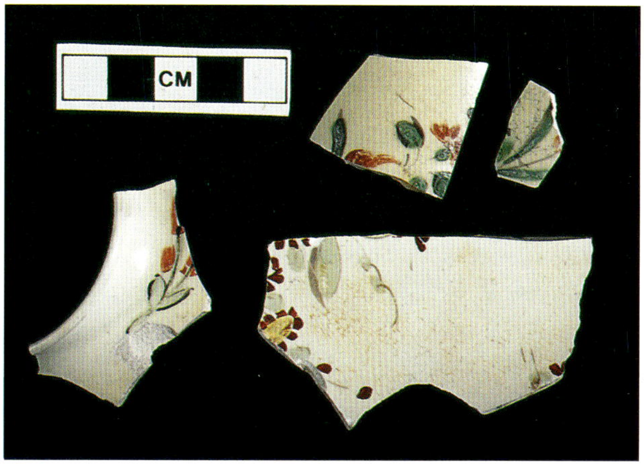

Plate 6. Overglaze-enamel decoration

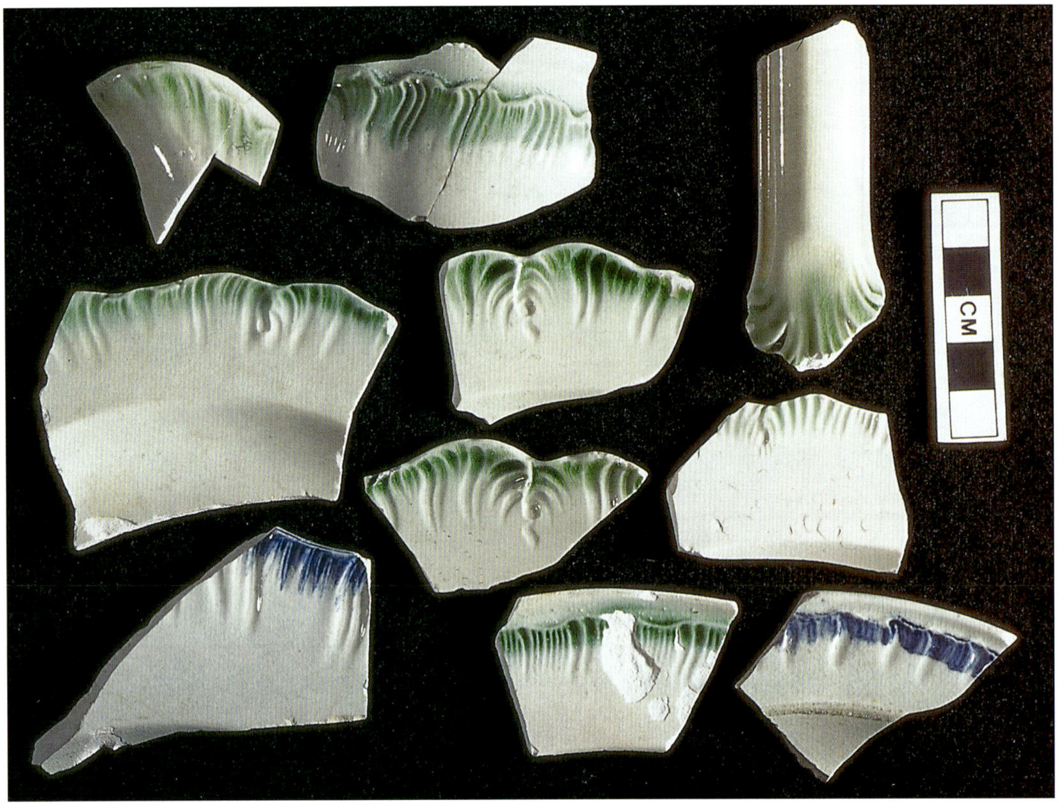

Plate 7. Blue and green 'Shell-edge' or 'Feather-edge' decoration

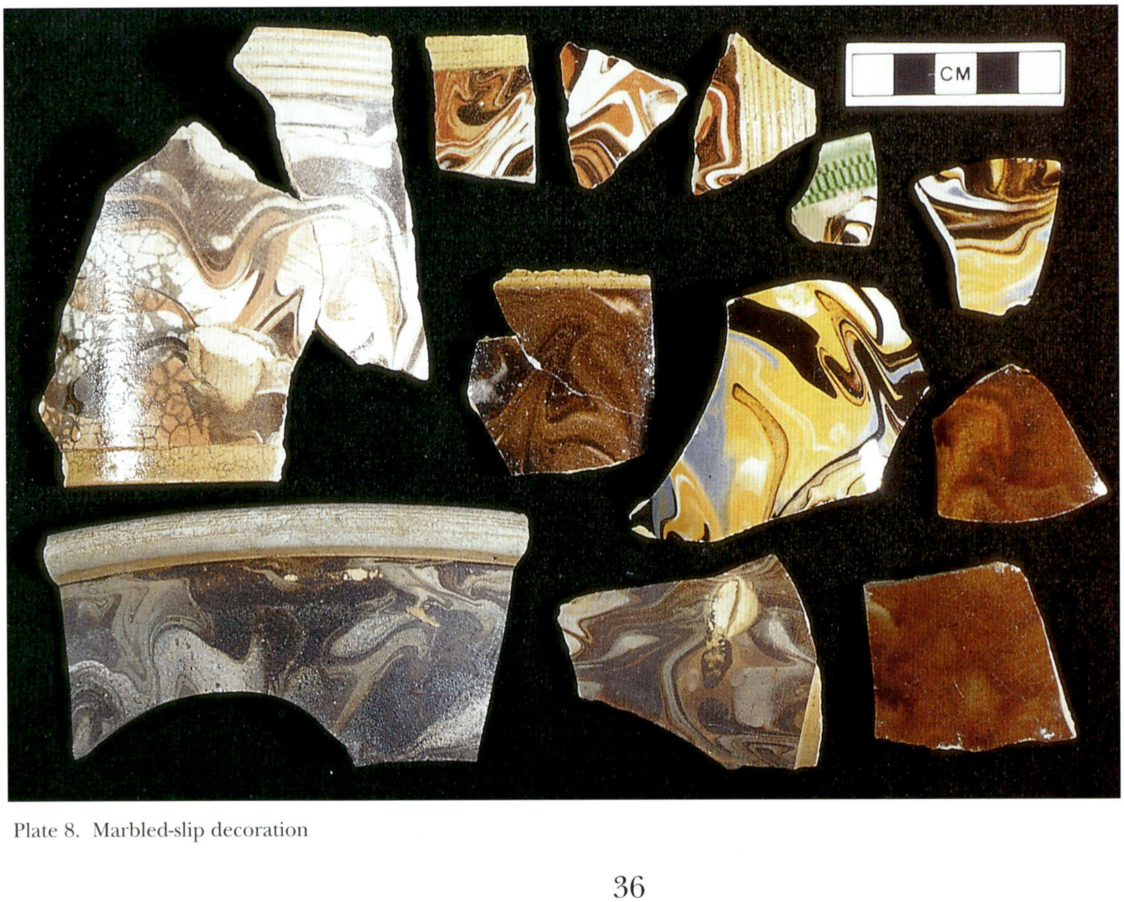

Plate 8. Marbled-slip decoration

Plate 9. 'Tortoiseshell' or 'Whieldon-type' decoration

Plate 10. Decorated pearlwares

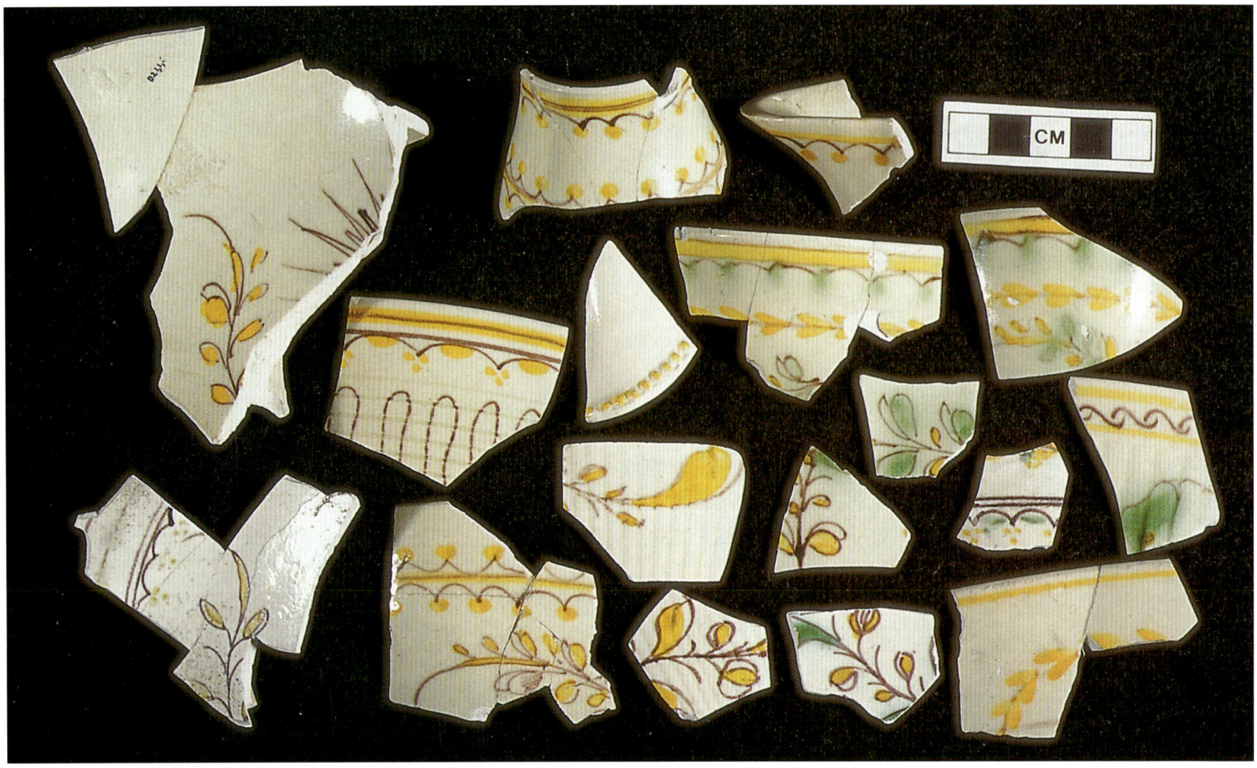

Plate 11. Yellow painted wares

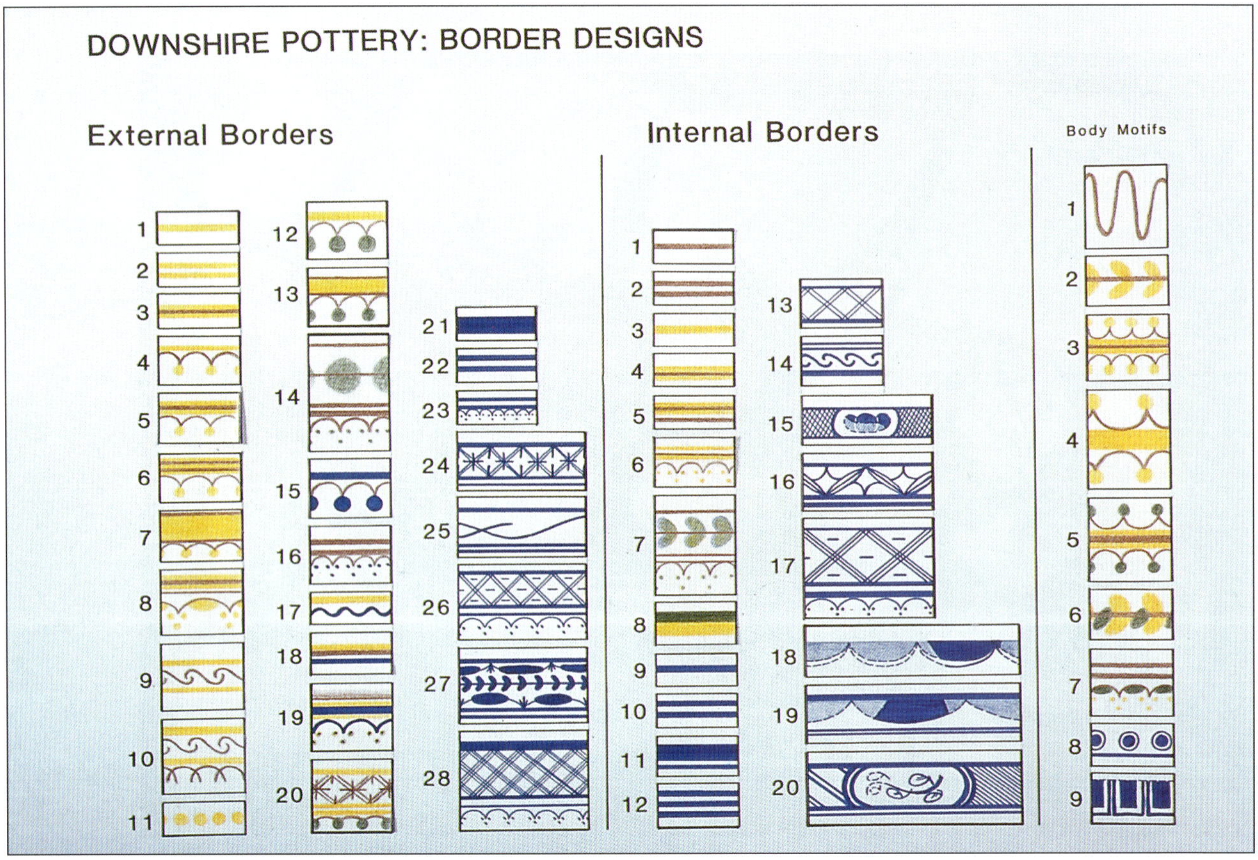

Plate 12. Schematic drawing of the full range of Downshire Pottery borders

Plate 13. Large monochrome-slip decorated baluster jugs attributed to the Downshire Pottery (see p 30)

Plate 14. Marble-slip decorated jugs attributed to the Downshire Pottery (see pp 30–31)

Plate 15. Two teapots attributed to the Downshire Pottery, on the basis of their moulded spouts and distinctive decoration

Plate 16. Verso of coffee-pot and sparrowbeak jug shown in Plate 20, with an attributed 'tortoiseshell'-decorated mug

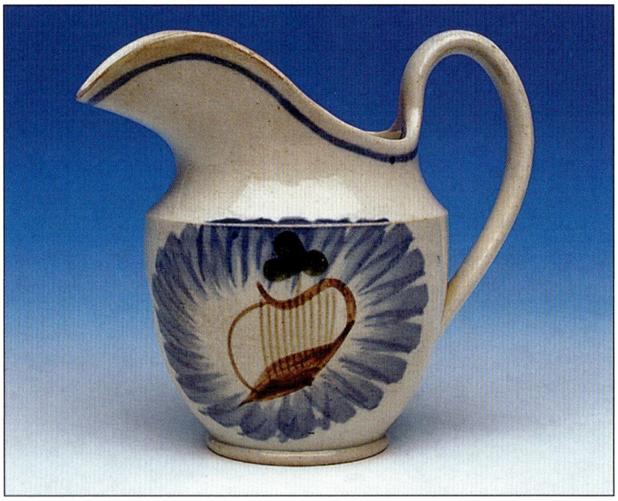

Plate 17. Small, helmet-shaped jug, with painted harp and shamrock design, attributed to the Downshire Pottery *after* 1800

Plate 18. 'Zebra' plate with harp and shamrock border, tentatively attributed to the Downshire Pottery *after* 1800

Plate 19. 'Stag' plate with harp and shamrock border, tentatively attributed to the Downshire Pottery *after* 1800

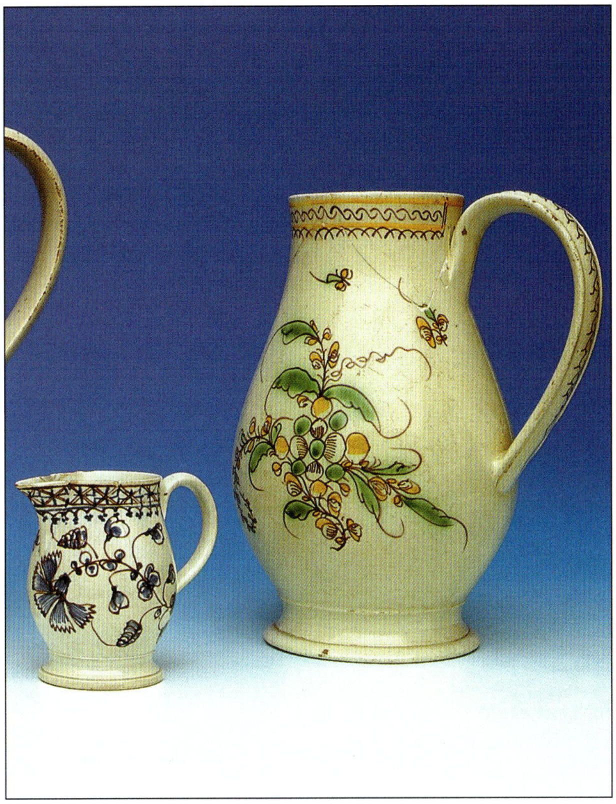

Plate 20. Downshire Pottery coffee-pot (spout missing) and sparrowbeak jug with painted sprig decoration

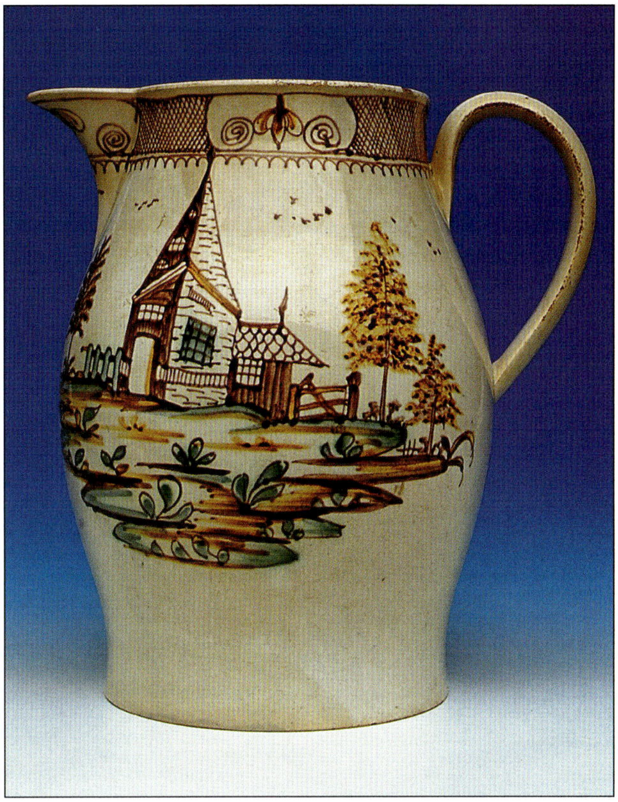

Plate 21. Large baluster jug attributed to the Downshire Pottery (see p 32)

Plate 22. Recently discovered pearlware plate. The style of decoration is very similar to that of the Downshire coffee-pot, (colour plate 20)

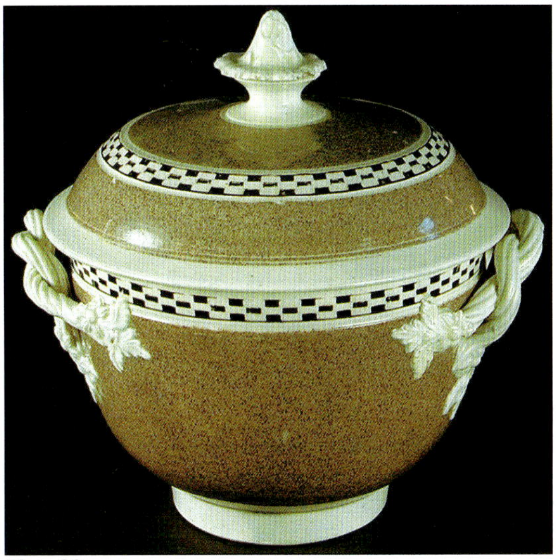

Plate 23

Plate 23a. Sugar-bowl and cover, attributed to the Downshire Pottery. The floral-sprig handle terminals are identical to excavated examples (see Figure 17ii, 24xvi and 24xvii)

Plate 23a

CATALOGUE, PART 2

Unglazed Fragments

Twenty-three different types of pottery object were recorded among the unglazed, biscuit-ware fragments, often in a variety of forms. In accordance with other catalogues of this type, these have been classified in alphabetical order.

In trying to reconstruct the range of wares produced by the Downshire Pottery we are fortunate that several printed catalogues have survived of comparable English creamware potteries of the period. These include, in full or in part, the catalogues of Wedgwood, the Leeds Pottery, the Don Pottery, the Whitehead Catalogue and the St Anthony's Pottery, Newcastle (see bibliography for references). Where relevant, illustrations from these catalogues have been inserted into the text to give a clearer impression of the wares that the Belfast potters were producing. The most readily available summary of the techniques employed in manufacturing creamware is published in David Barker's account of the William Greatbatch site (see bibliography).

Table 3.1 Catalogue of Unglazed Fragments

	Baking dishes	*– see plates*
	Basins	*– see plates*
1.	**Baskets**	
2.	**Beakers**	
	Bin-label	*– see vintner's bin label*
3.	**Bowls** *(other than tea bowls, ointment pots)*	
	Butter-boats	*– see sauce-boats*
4.	**Chamber pots**	
	Coffee cans	*– see mugs and tankards*
5.	**Coffee and hot-water pots**	
	Cream boats	*– see sauce-boats*
6.	**Cruets**	
	Cups	*– see tea bowls*
	Dessert plates	*– see plates*
	Dishes	*– see plates*
7.	**Eggcup**	
	Handle types	*– see diagnostic features*
	Hot-water pots	*– see coffee and hot-water pots*
8.	**Inkwell**	
	Jelly moulds*	
9.	**Jugs**	
	Knop types	*– see diagnostic features*
10.	**Ladles**	
	Lid types	*– see diagnostic features*
	Miniature tea-wares	*– see toy tea-wares*
11.	**Mugs and tankards**	
	Mustard pots**	*– see straight-sided vessels*
12.	**Ointment pots**	
13.	**Plates, platters and dishes**	
	Punch bowls	*– see bowls*
14.	**Sauce-boats**	
15.	**Saucers**	
	Soup dishes	*– see dishes*
	Spout types	*– see diagnostic features*
	Tankards	*– see mugs and tankards*
16.	**Straight-sided vessels**	
17.	**Sugar bowls**	
18.	**Tea bowls**	
19.	**Tea caddy/canister**	
20.	**Teapots**	
21.	**Toy tea-wares**	
	Tumblers	*– see beakers*
22.	**Tureens**	
23.	**Vintner's bin label**	
24.	**Diagnostic features (spouts, handles and lids)**	
25.	**Kiln furniture and associated objects**	

* The jelly moulds described here were not recovered by the excavations, hence they have not been given an excavation catalogue number. The attributions are instead based upon stylistic characteristics.

** Complete mustard pots were unrecorded. Some vessels described here as straight-sided vessels may represent 'mustard pots'.

1. BASKETS (Figs. 1i, 1ii)

These are recorded in plain creamware, but the height and diameter of the baskets is not known. This type of open, finely-woven creamware basket, referred to variously as a 'fruit basket' or 'strawberry dish' in contemporary accounts, appears to have been produced by most English creamware potteries during the late 18th and early 19th centuries. Despite their obvious fragility, comparatively large numbers have survived to the present day.

The two very small shards recovered (1i) bear no distinctive or diagnostic features of any kind, but they do at least confirm that such baskets were once made in Belfast. No fragments were found of the moulded, basket-woven oval plates upon which these baskets normally stood, (1ii), but it seems highly likely that these too were produced here.

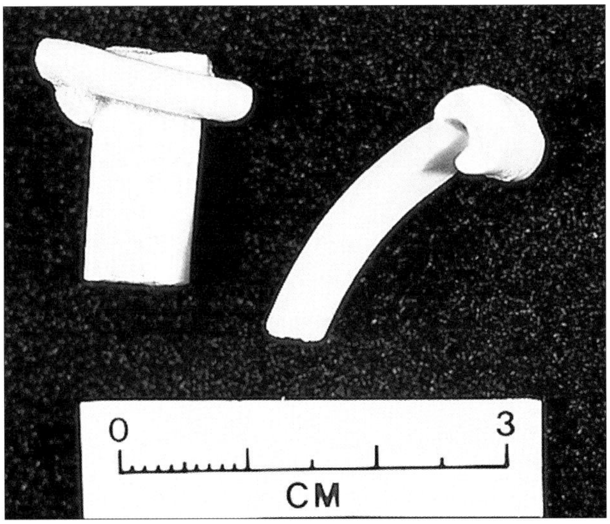

Fig.1i

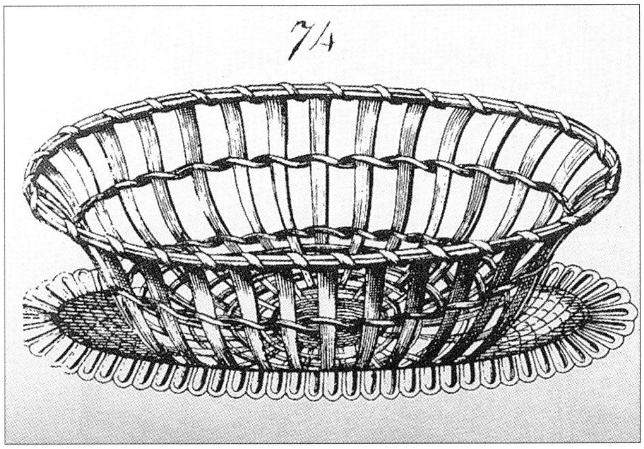

Fig.1ii Comparable basket illustrated by the *Don Pottery Catalogue*, No. 74 (1807).

2. BEAKERS (Fig. 2i)

Types of ware recorded:	Creamware, buff-bodied ware
Height:	85–90 mm
Rim Diameter:	72–75 mm
Footrim diameter:	50–53 mm
Footrim width:	2.5–5.0 mm
Body decoration:	Plain
Glaze decoration:	Brown and green 'tortoiseshell', dark brown marbled-slip
Full profiles recorded:	2

Utilitarian flared beakers, with straight or slightly convex sides, are now among the rarest of surviving creamware vessels, but they were excavated in some quantity. The principal form of glaze decoration appears to have been green-brown 'tortoiseshell' decoration, as illustrated, but it is also possible that some of the smaller brown/white marbled, buff-bodied shards recovered (see colour plate 8) are also beaker fragments.

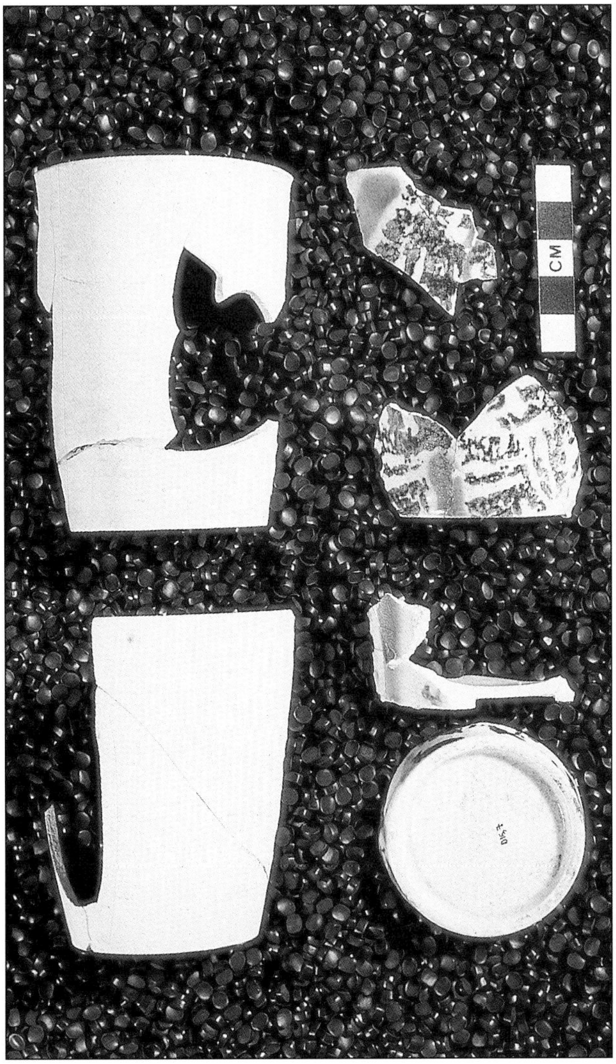

Fig.2i

3. BOWLS (Figs. 3i–3iv)

Biscuit-ware bowl fragments are grouped into three categories based on their decoration;

a. *Plain bowls* (3i);
b. *Bowls with incised bands* (3ii);
c. *Bowls with vertical ribs* (engine-turned) (3iii–iv).
(See also Tea Bowls, catalogue no 18.)

3a. Plain bowls (Fig. 3ii)

Types of ware recorded:	Creamware, pearlware, fine and course drabware
Height:	57–81 mm (average tea bowl 49mm)
Rim Diameter:	c. 100–300 mm
Footrim diameter:	c. 48–115 mm
Full profiles recorded:	3

3b. Bowls with incised bands (Fig. 3ii)

Types of ware recorded:	Creamware
Height:	55–80 mm (average tea bowl 49 mm)
Rim diameter:	c. 140–240 mm
Footrim diameter:	c. 50–110 mm
Full profiles recorded:	2

Wheel-thrown bowls, in a wide variety of profiles and sizes, were among the most common wasters encountered. Despite this variety, however, none of the many biscuitware fragments recovered appeared to exhibit any distinguishing characteristic. It may well transpire that examples of Belfast bowls will not be recognised on the basis of form alone.

A representative range of profiles, footrims and rim forms were collected, indicative of the various functions of the bowls produced. Plain rims occurred principally on decorative wares such as large punch-bowls, 'slop-bowls' and fruit-bowls, while the more utilitarian washing and baking basins often exhibit a reinforced folded or rolled rim (3i–ii). A wide variety of footrim types and sizes were also recorded, (whether tapering, vertical or flared, as 3ii top right), but once again, none of these more detailed characteristics appeared distinctive or diagnostic.

3c. Bowls with engine-turned ribbed decoration (Figs. 3iii and 3iv)

Types of ware recorded:	Creamware
Height:	c. 100 mm
Rim diameter:	c. 150 mm
Footrim diameter:	c. 70 mm
Full profiles recorded:	None

Fragments of at least three medium-sized bowls were recorded which exhibited fine, engine-turned vertical ribbing, (3iii), similar in style to the Don Pottery example published in 1807, (3iv). As with other Downshire Pottery bowls however, the form is not diagnostic; only the unusual yellow and brown painted floral decoration is distinctive.

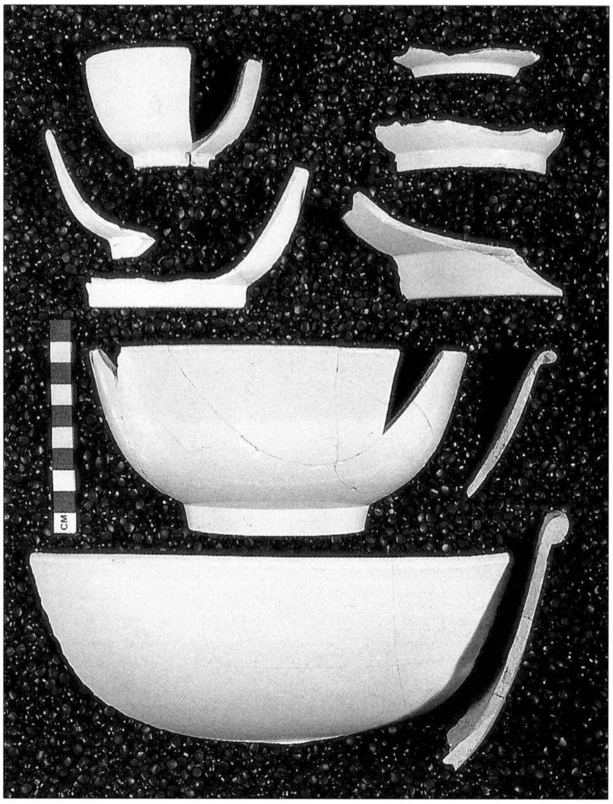

Fig.3i

Fig.3ii

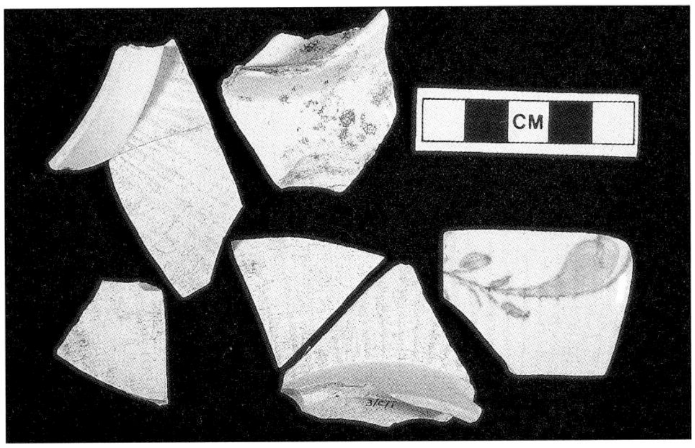

Fig.3iii

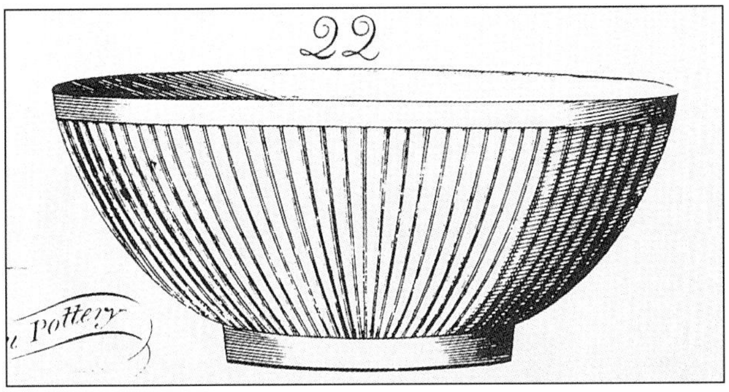

Fig.3iv

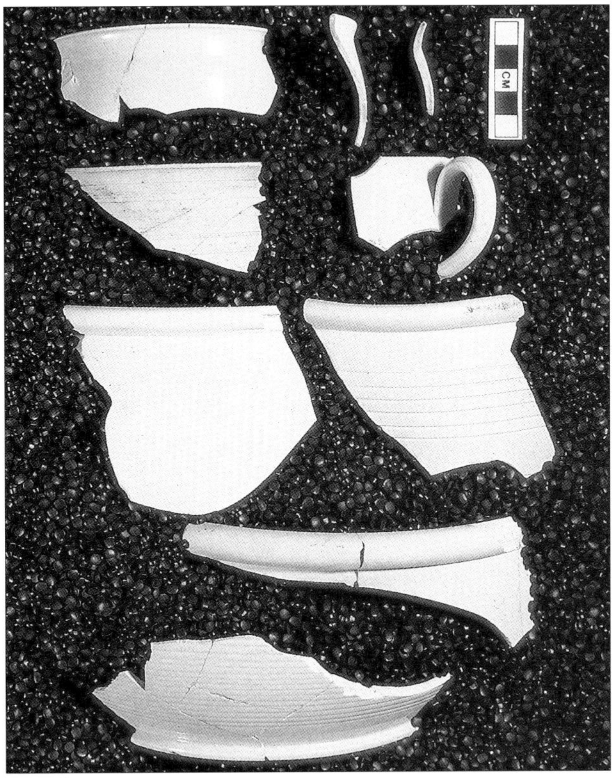

Fig.4i

4. CHAMBER POTS (Figs. 4i–4ii)

Height:	Unknown (no full profiles recorded)
Rim diameter:	Small: 110–130 mm, large: 160–220 mm
Footrim diameter:	Small: c. 75–90 mm, large: c. 130–160 mm
Body decoration:	Plain or with incised horizontal bands
Glaze decoration:	Two types recorded: 'tortoiseshell' (on creamware), dark brown marbled-slip (on buff-bodied ware)
Full profiles:	None

Two distinct sizes of 'chamber pot' were recorded; a small pot (c.110–130 mm rim diameter) with a slightly everted rim, and a larger 'full-size' chamber pot, (160–220 mm rim diameter), usually with a reinforced 'rolled' or folded rim. Creamware and buff-bodied ware versions were produced of both sizes. Although no full profiles were found, the excavated shards (4i) can be readily compared with intact (Irish or English) examples (4ii). Note that the different rims also match the Downshire finds.

The smaller version may have been a child's chamber pot, or more likely (to judge from the different type of rim) they were produced to serve a different function (a spitoon, for example, or perhaps they represent 'Porringers' or food bowls). No diagnostic forms were recorded, but it is worth noting that at least two decorated types were produced, with 'tortoiseshell' and marbled-slip decoration, sometimes with an additional embellishment of incised horizontal bands.

Fig.4ii

5. COFFEE AND HOT-WATER POTS (Figs. 5i–5iii)

(The spoutless coffee-pot illustrated is *attributed* to Belfast, rather than an excavated fragment.)

Types of ware recorded:	Creamware, pearlware
Height and rim diameter:	Unknown from excavated shards
Attributed coffee-pot:	Height: 210mm, rim diameter: 79 mm
Footrim diameter:	Excavated shards: 68–108 mm
Attributed coffee-pot:	110 mm
Body decoration:	Plain, engine-turned vertical ribs
Glaze decoration:	Only floral-sprig painting recorded, but other types probable
Full profiles recorded:	None

The broken and now spoutless coffee-pot shown (5i, top right, ii–iii), can be confidently attributed to Belfast by the style of its decoration (cf. shards shown in colour plate 11). Quite apart from the unusual and distinctive yellow, green and manganese painted decoration, the creamware of which it is made is distinctive – slightly over-fired to give the appearance of a hybrid white 'salt-glaze' (with orange-peel texture). The coffee-pot is discussed further in the 'Coloured Wares', p 32.

The piece also demonstrates how one new attribution can improve our understanding of the Downshire Pottery's wares. No full profiles of coffee-pots were recorded among the excavated wasters, even though the very robust bases were common. Were it not for the *attributed* coffee-pot their shape would not be known.

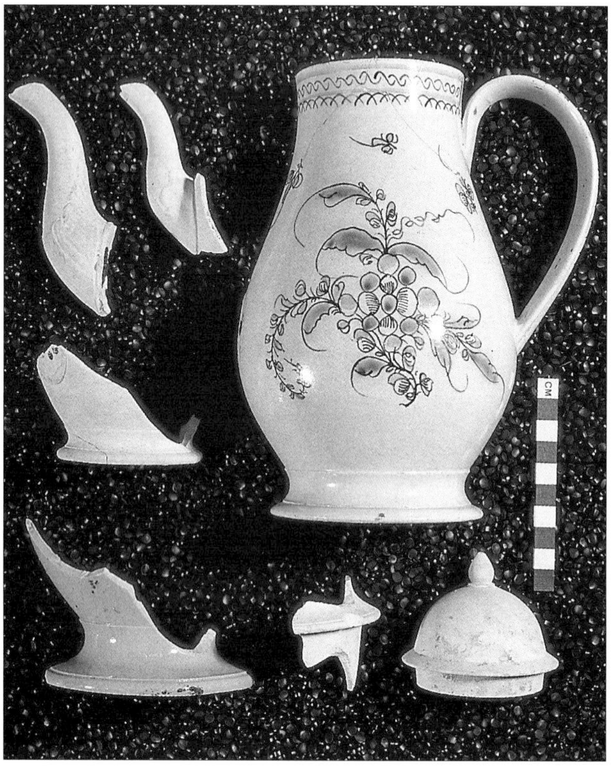

Fig.5i

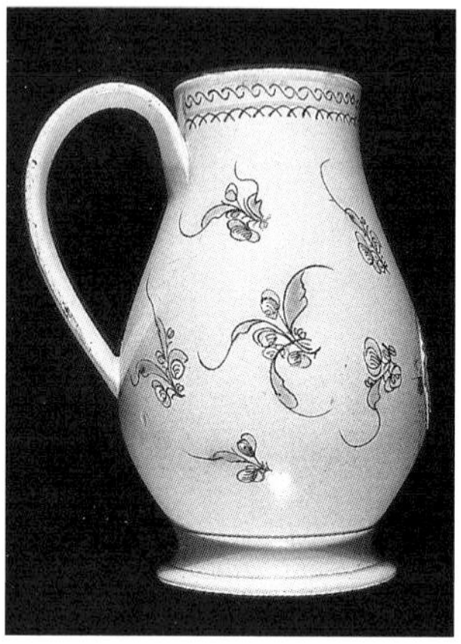
Fig.5ii

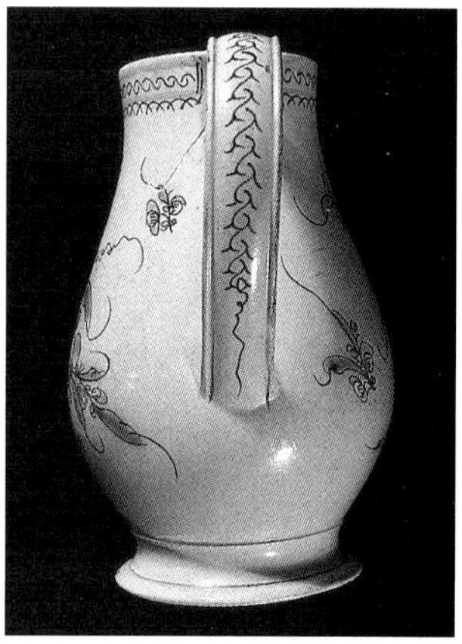
Fig.5iii

6. CRUETS (Figs. 6i–6ii)

Types of ware recorded:	Creamware
Height:	Unknown (no full profiles recorded). Comparable example 166 mm
Lip diameter:	36–46 mm
Footrim diameter:	44–46 mm
Body decoration:	Plain
Glaze decoration:	Plain creamware recorded only
Full profiles recorded:	None

(The example illustrated was purchased locally and is considered a probable example of Belfast manufacture, but no full profiles were recorded among the excavated wares.)

A small range of individually hand-thrown and pierced cruets fragments were recovered, (6i), their slightly varying sizes suggesting different functions (salt and pepper shakers, sugar sifters, etc).The separately made 'dome' portion on top varied most – sometimes plain, or with an edge-flange, or with a small tear-shaped knop. No decorated examples were found. The intact example shown here was purchased locally many years ago (formerly Angus MacDonald collection), and is indistinguishable from excavated fragments – it might well be a Downshire product.

As the Don Pottery catalogue indicates (6ii), these cruets were often sold in sets originally, although these are now extremely rare.

7. EGGCUP (Fig. 6i bottom right)

Types of ware recorded:	Creamware
Recorded forms:	1
Height:	Approximately 58 mm
Rim diameter:	40 mm
Footrim diameter:	40 mm
Footrim profile:	18 mm
Body and glaze decoration:	Plain creamware, some with incised line at junction of bowl and stem
Full profiles recorded:	None

Eggcup fragments proved extremely rare, with only three shards positively identified in total. All three are illustrated (6i: bottom right).

One of the two eggcup bowls bears an incised line at the junction with the stem (complementing the incised line on the foot) but otherwise the form appears to be entirely plain, with no distinguishing features of any kind to aid in the recognition of Downshire examples.

Fig.6i

Fig.6ii

8. INKWELL (Fig. 8i)

Types of ware recorded:	Pearlware
Dimensions:	64 x 55 mm, aperture 36 mm diameter (estimated)
Glaze decoration:	Painted manganese brown and cobalt blue flower sprigs
Full profiles recorded:	None

The small shard illustrated (8i) has a flat profile (4 mm thick) and an inner edge which is obviously circular, suggesting that this is almost certainly an inkwell fragment. It is impossible to speculate further; the main purpose of recording such a tiny shard is simply that it may assist in identifying an intact example.

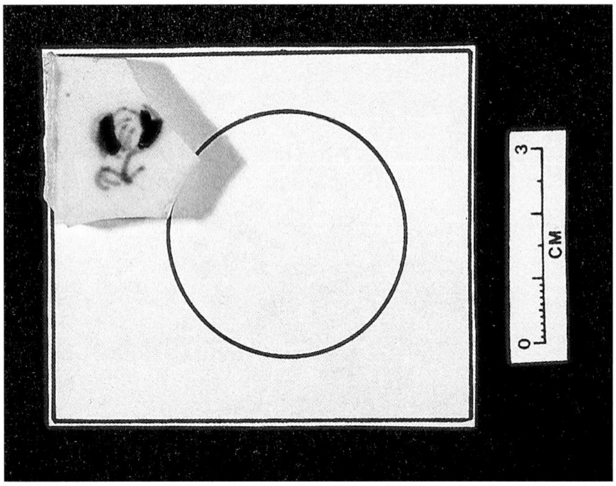

Fig.8i

JELLY MOULDS (Figs. JMi–JMii)

Types of ware recorded:	Creamware
Examples recorded by excavation:	None
Dimensions:	'Sparrow': 82 x 69 mm, 52 mm deep 'Crayfish': 110 x 81 mm, 29 mm deep 'Fish':164 x 127 mm, 72 mm deep 'Asparagus': 175 x 97 mm, 52 mm deep

No fragments of creamware jelly moulds were found during the 1993 excavation (hence they possess no corresponding catalogue number). Even so, a number of such moulds are presently attributed tentatively to the Downshire Pottery on stylistic and other grounds.

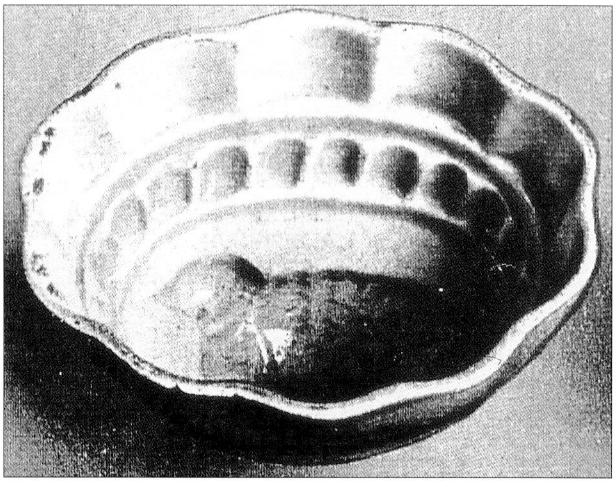

Fig.JMi

Fig.JMii

The distinguished Belfast historian RM Young first recovered shards of Downshire material on the pottery site in 1896, which in turn prompted him to form a collection of any surviving examples of Downshire ware that he could find. Young succeeded in gathering up a variety of creamware objects, some of which originally appear to have possessed a strong Belfast provenance – to judge from his written accounts. Sadly however, while many of the pieces which he identified are still known today, their all-important provenance details have since been lost.

In 1913, MSD Westropp's *Notes on the Pottery Manufacture in Ireland* included a photograph (Figure 13, p 14) which showed three of the shards that Young had collected on the pottery site in 1896, alongside which appeared a 'jelly mould of creamware said to have been made at the Downshire Pottery' (JMi). This mould – which shows a 'sparrow' or similarly small bird on a nest – is now in the Ulster Museum, together with other pieces from the Young collection. Among these is an obviously related jelly mould featuring a 'crayfish'. (JMii, front).

Now that the provenance of these two pieces has been lost Young's attribution to Belfast would appear weak, were it not for a second example of the 'sparrow' mould in another local collection (in Comber, County Down) which independently bears a late 19th-century label of attribution to the Downshire Pottery. Perhaps the best supporting evidence to date however, derives from the more recent discovery in Belfast of another jelly mould, this time bearing a 'fish' design, (JMii, top) which seems to form part of the same series. This mould is highly over-fired and of extremely unusual character, the body and glaze sharing very strong affinities with the distinctive Downshire coffee-pot (5i–iii). The fact that this design of 'fish' mould also appears to be unrecorded by specialist 'jelly mould' collectors in England adds support to its Belfast attribution – possibly even to a Belfast attribution for this group of moulds as a whole. There are certainly stylistic similarities between them all.

For now, as not even one fragment of a jelly mould was found by the excavations, the attribution of these jelly moulds to the Downshire Pottery should be judged cautiously, but the 'fish' mould in particular does seem to be a reasonable candidate.

9. JUGS (Figs. 9i–9x)

Five different shapes of jug were recorded, and will be examined in turn.

9a Sparrowbeak
9b Silver-shaped (pedestal-based)
9c Baluster
9d Barrel-shaped
9e Complex-moulded

9a. Sparrowbeak jugs (Fig. 9i, top row)

Height:	75–78 mm
Rim diameter:	40–46 mm
Footrim diameter:	36 mm
Body decoration:	Plain
Glaze decoration:	Green 'tortoiseshell', yellow-brown painted
Full profiles recorded:	2

Two slightly different forms were recorded – one with an undercut 'pedestal' base (see colour plate 20, left), the other with a simple rounded form. While only incomplete pieces of the first type were excavated (they are not illustrated here), a full biscuit-ware profile was recorded of the second form, (9i, top left), as well as several *near* profiles bearing splashed 'tortoiseshell' green, and painted yellow/brown dotted border motifs, (9i, top centre and right, see also colour plates 3 and 11).

None were found to exhibit any distinctive mouldings, (all of the handle terminations were plain, for example). Thus, despite the fact that the form of the small jug shown in colour plate 20 was recovered on the excavation, the attribution is principally based on the style of decoration.

9b. Silver-shaped (pedestal-based) (Fig. 9i, bottom row, 9ii and 9iii)

Height:	Size 1: 120 mm Size 2: approximately 250–300 mm
Rim diameter:	Size 1: 52–5 mm Size 2: approximately 120–30 mm
Footrim diameter:	Size 1: 56–8 mm Size 2: 130 mm
Body decoration:	Plain, moulded vertical ribbing
Glaze decoration:	Plain
Full profiles recorded:	2 (size 1 only)

The form of these jugs is perhaps most easily seen in the illustration from the Don Pottery catalogue (9ii). Two very distinct sizes of silver-shaped jug were recovered; a small version of about five inches height (probably for table use), and a much larger jug of c. 10 inches (probably a water jug). No examples were found with decorated glazes – all were plain, white creamware, but an intact example of the version which bears vertical moulded ribbing (9iii) would be a handsome piece of pottery nonetheless.

Fig.9i

Fig.9ii

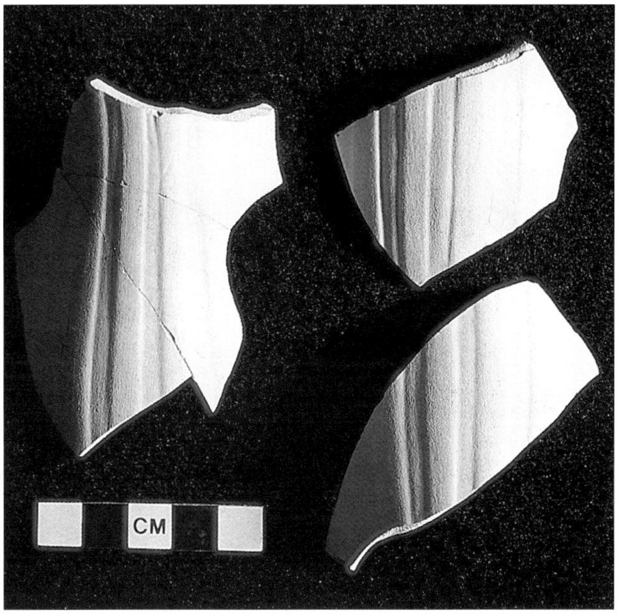

Fig.9iii

9c. Baluster jugs (Fig. 9iv)

Height:	Very variable. Minimum 140 mm, maximum > 250 mm (estimated)
Rim diameter:	Minimum 80 mm, maximum c.175 mm
Footrim diameter:	Minimum 80 mm, maximum c.175 mm
Body decoration:	Plain
Glaze decoration:	All types
Full profiles recorded:	2 (small size only, 140 mm height)

The plain-bodied baluster jugs were among the most common vessels recorded. However, with the exception of certain spout and handle mouldings (discussed and illustrated in more detail in the 'diagnostic features' section, pp 75–78), there is nothing distinctive in the form of any of them. Several baluster jugs have been attributed to Downshire, but in each case, the attribution is based upon the style of decoration rather than the form (front cover, colour plates 13, 14 and 21).

The baluster and barrel-shaped jug fragments together exhibited the widest variety of decorative styles of any group recorded. Among the excavated wares, plain creamware was probably most common. (These would either have been sold in plain white or perhaps with added, overglaze decoration.) Others exhibited 'tortoiseshell' glazes (9iv, lower left, colour plate 9), blue marbled-slips (9iv, lower right, colour plate 8), yellow/brown painted borders (9iv, centre right) and brown monochrome slips with incised lines (colour plate 2, centre top).

Fig.9iv

9d. Barrel-shaped jugs (Figs. 9v–9viii)

Height:	Very variable. Minimum 110 mm, maximum > 250 mm (estimated)
Rim diameter:	Minimum 70 mm, maximum > 160 mm
Footrim diameter:	Minimum 70 mm
Body decoration:	Plain, engine-turned vertical ribbing and borders, incised horizontal bands
Glaze decoration:	Various, predominantly slip-decorated
Full profiles recorded:	None

Like baluster jugs, barrel-shaped jugs were common among the excavated assemblage, but there are few characteristics in their form that can be considered truly distinctive. Some acanthus-moulded spouts are described in more detail under 'diagnostic features'.

A noticeable difference between the baluster jugs (which were only made in creamware) and the barrel-shaped jugs, is that the latter were produced in both creamware and buff-bodied ware, reflecting their more utilitarian character (9v, lower). They were also usually slip-decorated rather than painted, both with plain slips (9v, upper) and marbled slips (9v, centre and bottom), often enhanced with incised horizontal bands and borders. Just a few additional details are worthy of remark.

The first is an unusual style of 'combed' decoration that was noted on one of the monochrome-slip jugs (9vi). This style of decoration has not been observed among the excavated wares from other pottery sites.

Only one of the marbled-slip decorated shards recovered – probably from a barrel-shaped jug – exhibits an engine-turned or rouletted border, which has been distinctively highlighted in green (9vii). The border style and green colour are strikingly similar in appearance to a marble slip-trailed barrel jug which was purchased at auction in Belfast in 1996 (colour plate 14). As only one green-decorated shard was recovered during the excavation, however, there is a slight possibility that it represents outside contamination – otherwise this would be one of the firmest attributions to the Downshire Pottery to date. (Comparable jugs were certainly made in England at the same time.)

A small barrel-shaped jug purchased in Greyabbey, County Down in 1997 exemplifies the difficulties that arise when attempting to attribute examples of this rather undistinguished shape. The machine-turning, form, and painted-border design were all recorded among the excavated assemblage. But even with this degree of correspondence, the lack of any truly distinctive feature still means that we cannot positively tell if the jug is English or Irish.

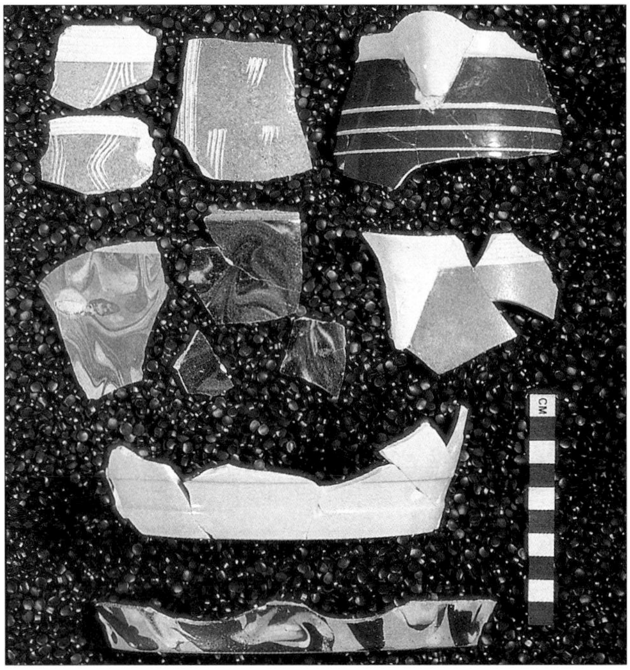

Fig.9v

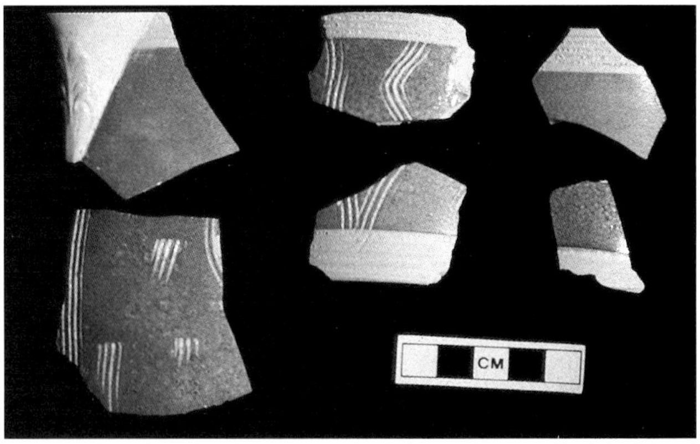

Fig.9vi

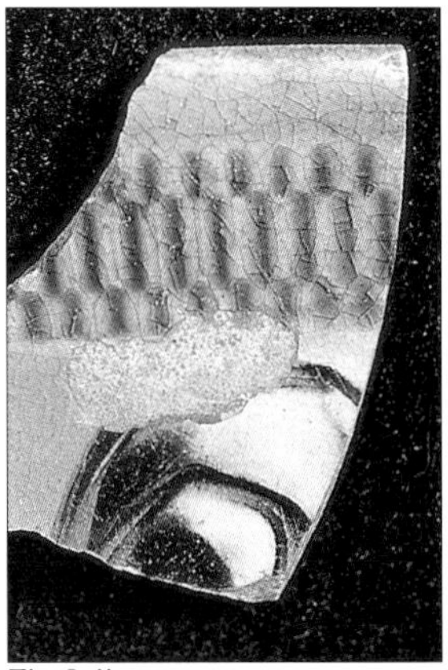

Fig.9vii

Fig. 9viii

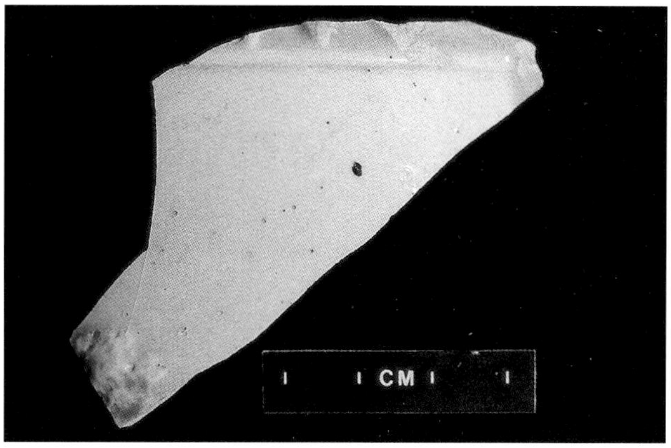

Fig.9ix

Fig.9x

9e. Complex-moulded Jugs (Figs. 9ix–9x)

This over-fired fragment (9ix) is perhaps the most enigmatic and interesting of all of the shards recorded by the excavation – it is a great shame that no more fragments were found. The form is obvious – the shard comes from a type of figurative, relief-moulded jug which is more commonly found decorated in 'Pratt-type' colours (9 x). Rather unfortunately in this case, the moulding only shows a portion of foliage, highlighted with light green glaze, although a section of the upper, moulded border is also visible, flaring out towards the spout (top right).

As might be imagined, the existence of this unusually complex shard among the Downshire assemblage gave rise to much searching through books and catalogues for similar examples. Unexpectedly, despite the fact that the form is reasonably common, (with many minor variations), no precise matches were found anywhere in the literature.

10. LADLES (Fig. 10i)

Types of ware recorded:	Pearlware, creamware
Forms recorded:	1
Body decoration:	Moulded linear decoration (see creamware example)
Glaze decoration:	Blue-line painting on pearlware examples
Full profiles recorded:	None

Several fragments of a single design of moulded ladle handle were recorded, (10i) but were insufficient to indicate, even approximately, the size or shape of an intact example. No fragments of ladle bowls were recorded.

The plain creamware fragment illustrated (bottom left) shows most clearly the complex moulded linear decoration of these handles. On pearlware examples, (top and centre) this moulded decoration was picked out in cobalt blue and further enhanced with blue-line cross-hatching.

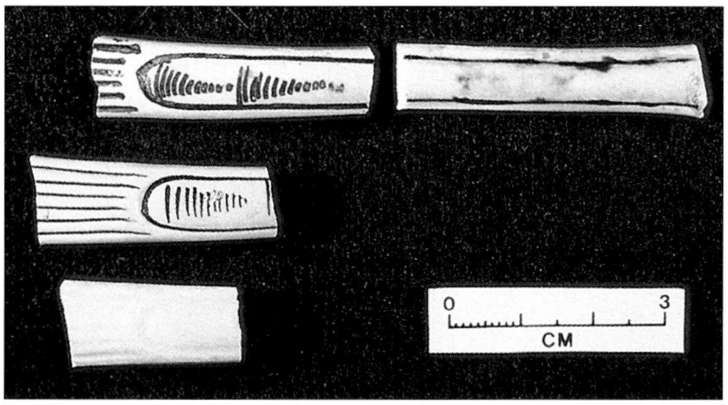

Fig.10i

11. MUGS AND TANKARDS (Figs. 11i–11iii)

Number of forms recorded:	1 (of widely varying sizes)
Types of ware recorded:	Creamware, pearlware, fine and coarse buff-bodied ware
Size range:	Rim/footrim diameter 40–100 mm
Height range:	Approximately 60–150 mm (estimated)
Body decoration:	Plain, incised horizontal bands, incised lines at rim and footrim, complex floral handle terminations
Glaze decoration:	Plain, floral painted,'Chinese landscape', tortoiseshell, monochrome slips, marbled slips, overglaze enamels
Full profiles recorded:	> 6

Recorded profiles of Downshire's mugs and tankards (11i) range from the very small (estimated c.50 mm height), to the very tall (estimated 180 mm or more), with an average height of about 120 mm (just under five inches).

Despite their abundance and the wide range of decorative styles encountered, there are actually very few characteristics among the Downshire mugs and tankards that can be considered 'diagnostic'. A large number of mugs – buff-bodied examples with a monochrome or marbled slip decoration especially – bear incised lines on the rim and around the base (11i, bottom row). Others were produced in plain creamware with incised line decoration (11i, centre). The only potentially 'diagnostic' type present in the entire assemblage, however, is the single example which bears an applied flower sprig and traces of a double entwined handle, decorated simply with a red-brown monochrome slip (11i, centre right, and 11iii). Both the flower sprig and double entwined handle are discussed further in diagnostic features, p 76.

In addition to these excavated shards, two intact mugs are presently attributed to the Downshire Pottery: a small, plain white example in the Ulster Museum (from the RM Young collection), and a larger tortoiseshell tankard in the author's collection, purchased locally (11ii). The Ulster Museum example is entirely undistinguished and without provenance, so that it is impossible to comment on its attribution, but the larger tortoiseshell mug does appear to be of unusual colour when compared to English examples. Precise colour matches were found with excavated 'tortoiseshell' shards, suggesting that this tankard might well have been made by the Downshire Pottery, but with such a comparatively plain and simple form it is impossible to be certain.

Fig.11i

Fig.11ii

Fig.11iii

12. OINTMENT POTS (Figs. 12i–12ii)

Number of forms recorded:	2 (one with footrim, one without)
Types of ware recorded:	Creamware, fine buff-bodied ware
Height:	40 mm to approximately 120 mm (estimated)
Rim diameter:	30 mm to approximately 100 mm
Footrim diameter:	13–84 mm
Body decoration:	Plain, with folded or rolled rim
Glaze decoration:	None
Full profiles recorded:	2 (complete example also recorded by RM Young, 1896)

Large numbers of these small, thinly potted vessels (12i) were found during the excavation, but despite this their precise function remains a mystery. The only published examples located by the author appear in a recent American ceramic publication, in which such vessels are called 'custard cups' (*Collecting Yellow Ware*, LS McAllister and JL Michel, Paducah, Kentucky, 1993, pp 63–6). Inexplicably, however, it has been impossible to find even one intact example of these vessels in any museum collection, private collection or antique shop in recent years – all the more unexpected in view of the very large numbers that turned up on the Downshire site.

It is certainly possible that some of these vessels were 'custard cups', as the American authors suggest, but considering their continuous gradation in size from about one to four inches and their wholly undecorated, utilitarian appearance, it seems much more likely that they represent some form of ointment pot. Although some are very finely potted (for example 12i, centre right, second from top), they all possess a reinforced, rolled or folded rim which may have served as a 'string rim', for tying-on a parchment or cloth cover. The most obvious comparable objects are 17th and 18th-century delftware 'ointment pots', which are similar in general form and of comparable sizes, but the apparent rarity of surviving creamware examples is certainly anomalous.

An intact example was recovered from the Downshire site by RM Young in 1896, and was illustrated by Westropp in 1913, but its present whereabouts are unknown (12ii).

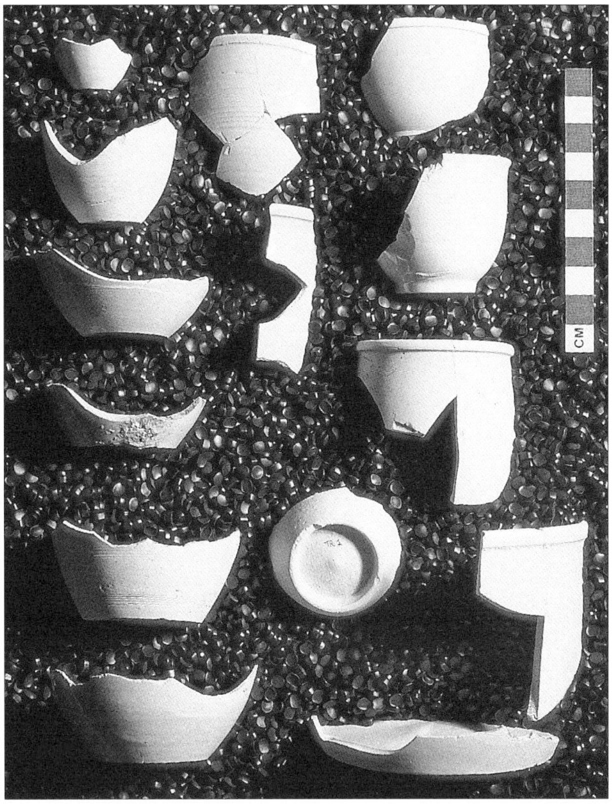

Fig.12i

Fig.12ii

13. PLATES, PLATTERS AND DISHES (Figs. 13i–13xv)

General observations
Flatwares in their various forms (plates, platters, soup dishes, baking dishes and shallow basins) were recovered in abundance. The range of all of the recorded forms and their essential dimensions are summarised in Table 3.2, page 57. As this table illustrates, six different moulded border designs were recorded on Downshire Pottery flatwares, of three distinct types:

1. **Plain borders** ('Bath' and 'Royal' patterns)
2. **'Shell' borders** ('scalloped' and 'wavy-edged' shell patterns)
3. **'Overlapped-shell' borders**, types A and B.

At first glance, some of these different types can appear very similar (for example, the two 'shell-edged' designs present), but on closer examination differences are evident. All of the flatwares were of creamware, with the exception of a small number of buff-bodied, deep oval baking dishes.

The patterns recorded are best understood simply from the illustrations, but a few broader remarks may assist future attributions. No flatwares were found with any form of backmark. It was not expected that factory marks would be found, but it was surprising that not even impressed numbers were present (indicating the size of the dish). These are a reasonably common feature on pearlware and creamware platters especially, so their absence is noteworthy. In addition, all of the circular flatwares excavated – the dinner plates and soup dishes – possessed a small, rounded footrim. Finally, none of the flatwares other than the circular types possessed any kind of footrim.

1. Plain borders

'Bath' pattern
This border, with a slightly upturned edge, was recorded on all types of flatware except oval baking dishes.

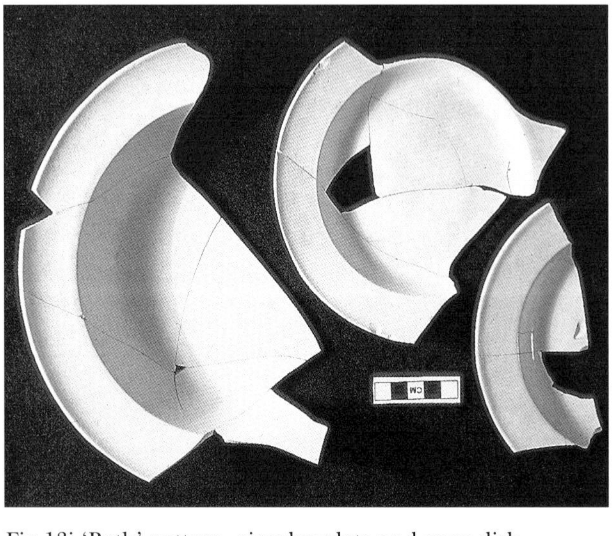

Fig.13i 'Bath' pattern, circular plate and soup-dish fragments

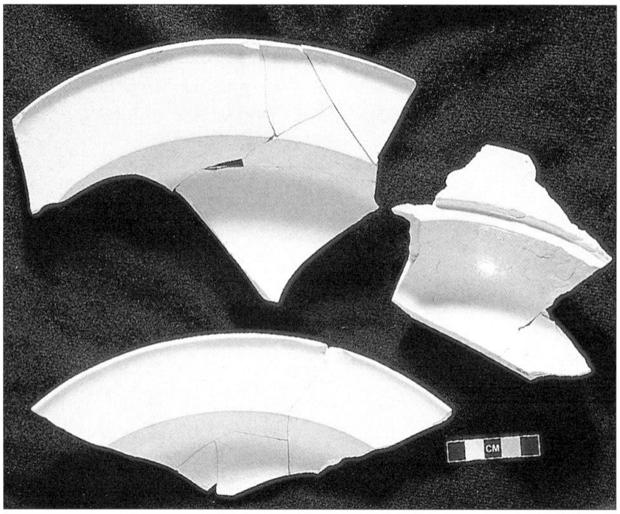

Fig.13ii 'Bath' pattern oval platters

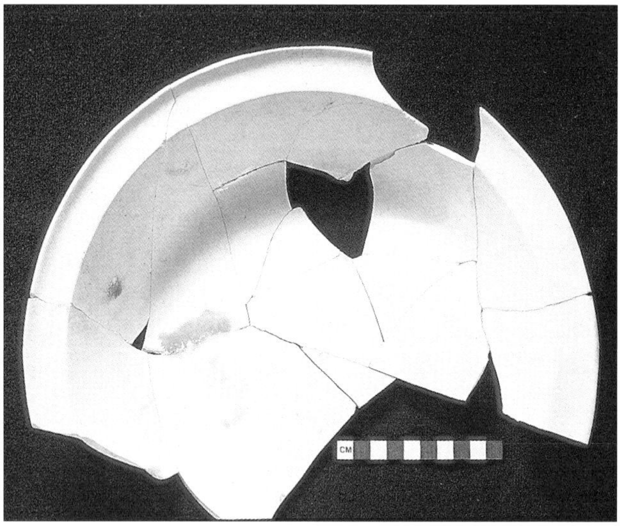

Fig.13iii 'Bath' pattern circular basin fragment

Fig.13iv 'Bath' pattern circular basin (private collection)

Table 3.2 Downshire Pottery: flatware types and dimensions

Pattern	Circular plates			Soup dishes	Squared-oval platters				Step-rim platters		Circular basins	Oval baking dishes		
	Small	Medium	Large	Large	Small	Medium	Large	V Large	Medium	Large	Large	Small	Medium	Large
Plain ('Bath')														
	D175	D210	–	D250	–	–	360x460*	390x485*	–	–	D320–30	–	–	–
	R25	R30	–	R32	R26	R38	R45–7	R50	R30	R32	R24	–	–	–
	H16	H19	–	H38	H20	H23	H30	H46	–	H54	H55	–	–	–
Scalloped ('Royal')														
	D180	–	D240	D240	–	–	–	–	–	–	–	–	–	–
	R20	R26	R30	R30	–	–	–	–	–	–	–	–	–	–
	H17	–	H20	H36	–	–	–	–	–	–	–	–	–	–
Scalloped shell														
	D160	D210	–	–	–	–	–	–	–	–	–	–	–	–
	R22	R26	–	–	–	–	–	–	–	–	–	–	–	–
	H14	H22	–	–	–	–	–	–	–	–	–	–	–	–
Wavy-edged shell – Type A														
	–	–	D260	D260	–	–	–	–	–	–	–	–	–	–
	–	–	R32	R28	–	–	–	–	R27	R30	–	–	–	–
	–	–	H21	H38	–	–	–	–	–	–	–	–	–	–
Wavy-edged shell – Type B														
	–	–	D260	–	–	–	–	–	–	–	–	–	–	–
	–	–	R30	–	R28	R36	R48	–	–	–	–	–	–	–
Overlapped shell – Plain Margin														
	–	–	H21	–	H20	–	–	–	–	–	–	–	–	–
	–	D200	D240	–	–	–	–	–	–	–	–	–	–	–
	–	R27	R32	–	–	–	–	–	–	–	–	–	–	–
	–	H20	H20	–	–	–	–	–	–	–	–	–	–	–
Overlapped Shell – Lapped Margin														
	–	–	–	–	–	–	–	–	–	–	–	–	320x240*	450x290*
	–	–	–	–	–	–	–	–	–	–	–	R16	R20	R20–30
	–	–	–	–	–	–	–	–	–	–	–	H45	H48	H58

* Approximate width and breadth dimensions estimated from comparative objects, not measured from excavated material.

D= diameter (mm) H= height (mm) R= rim width (mm)

'Bath' pattern continued

13i Circular plates and soup dishes
13ii Oval platters (some recessed for lids)
13iii Circular basin (excavated)
13iv Circular basin (private collection, Newtownabbey, County Antrim, diameter 320 mm)

'Royal' or 'scalloped' pattern
Only plates and soup dishes were recorded in this design, but it is highly likely that circular or oval platters would also have formed part of a complete dinner set.

13v Excavated small and medium-sized plates, and a soup dish (top)
13vi 'Royal' plate and two styles of platter (Ulster Museum and author's collection)
13vii Small fragment of deep dish, probably part of a 'Royal' pattern service
13viii Pattern of similar shape to 13vii from the Don Pottery catalogue (1807)

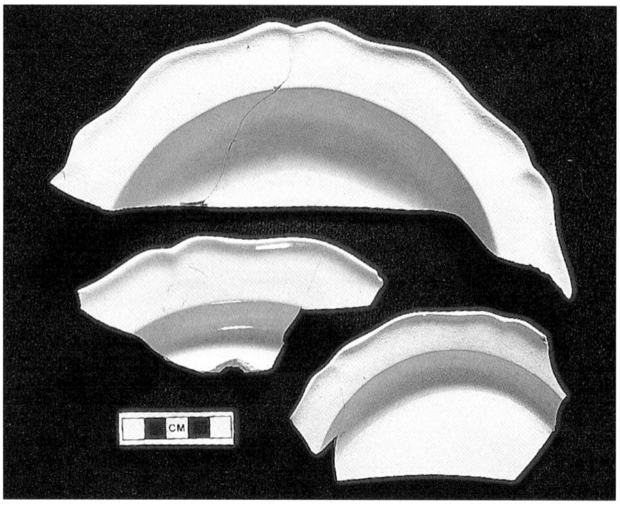

Fig.13v 'Royal' pattern dinner and side plate fragments

Fig.13vi 'Royal' pattern dinner plate, oval platter and circular platter, author's and Ulster Museum collections

2. 'Shell' borders

(Although this style of border is frequently described as 'feather-edged' in modern literature, several contemporary catalogues illustrate this as 'Shell' pattern.)

13ix Small side-plate 'Shell' border with 'scalloped' edge (ie, with six-fold symmetry, similar to the 'Royal' or 'scalloped' plain plates above)
13x Medium dinner plate, 'Shell' border with 'wavy-edge' (ie, irregular edge, no evident symmetry), type A
13xi Large dinner plate border fragments, 'Shell' border with 'wavy-edge', type B
13xii Platter border fragments, 'Shell' border with 'wavy-edge'.
See also colour plate 7 for glazed, coloured examples of these borders with green and blue (as above).

3. 'Overlapped shell' borders

Two slightly different styles of this design were recorded, on baking dishes and oval platters only. (They do not appear to occur on dinner plates.)

13xiii Oval baking dish, border type A
13xiv Border type A (detail)
13xv Border type B (oval dish fragments)

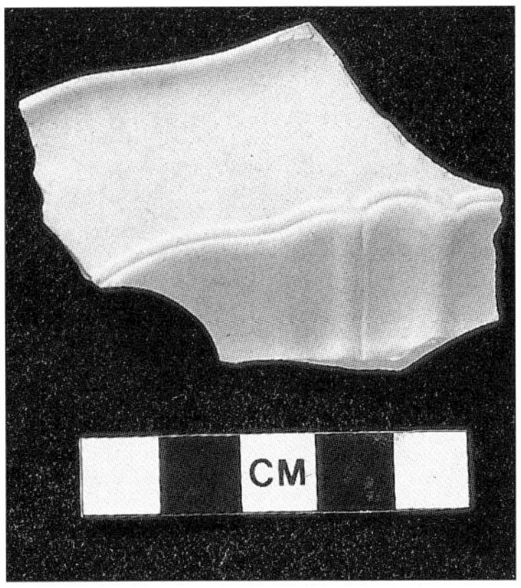

Fig.13vii 'Royal' pattern deep dish

Fig.13viii 'Royal' pattern deep dish, of similar form to the excavated fragment in Fig. 13vii. From the Don Pottery catalogue (1807)

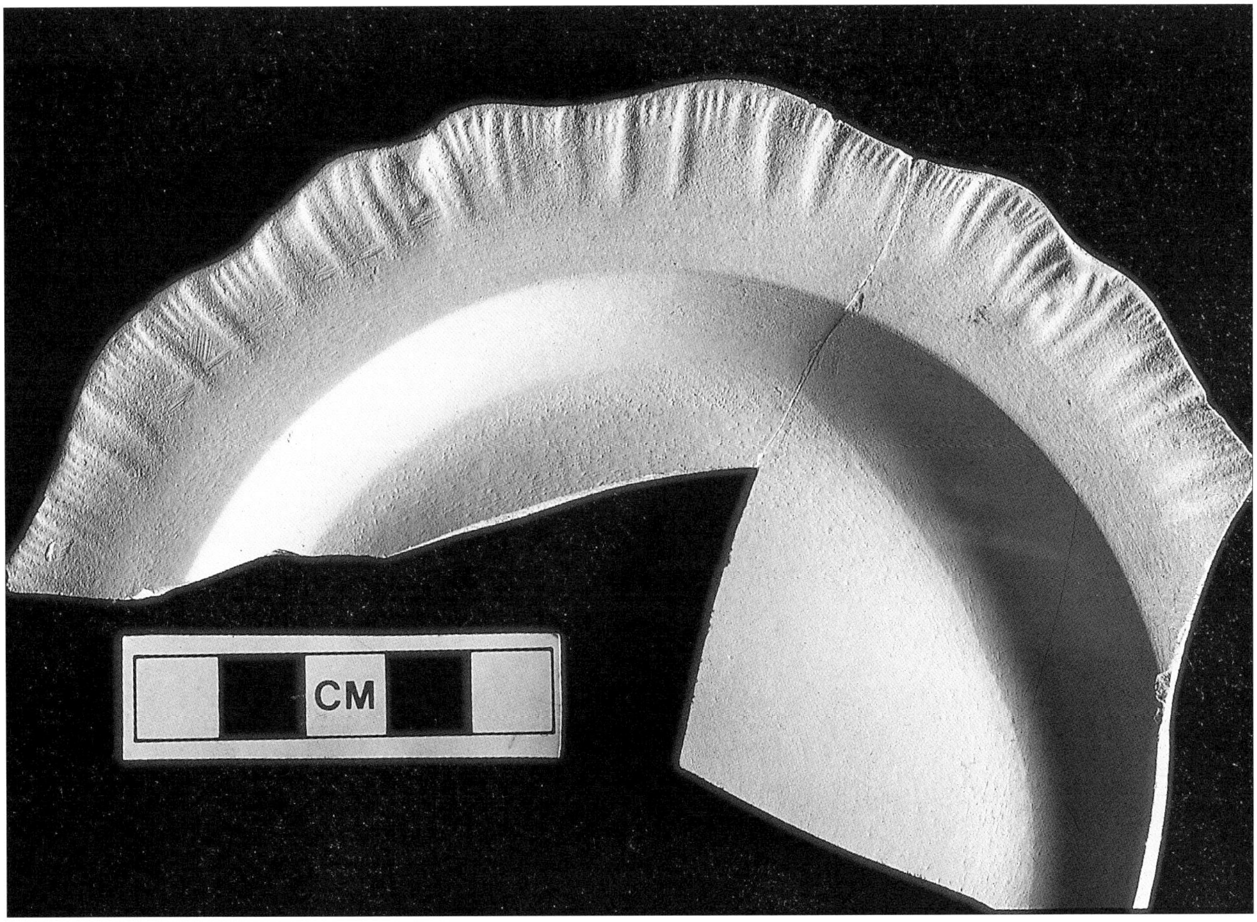

Fig.13ix Small side plate, 'Shell' border with 'scalloped' edge

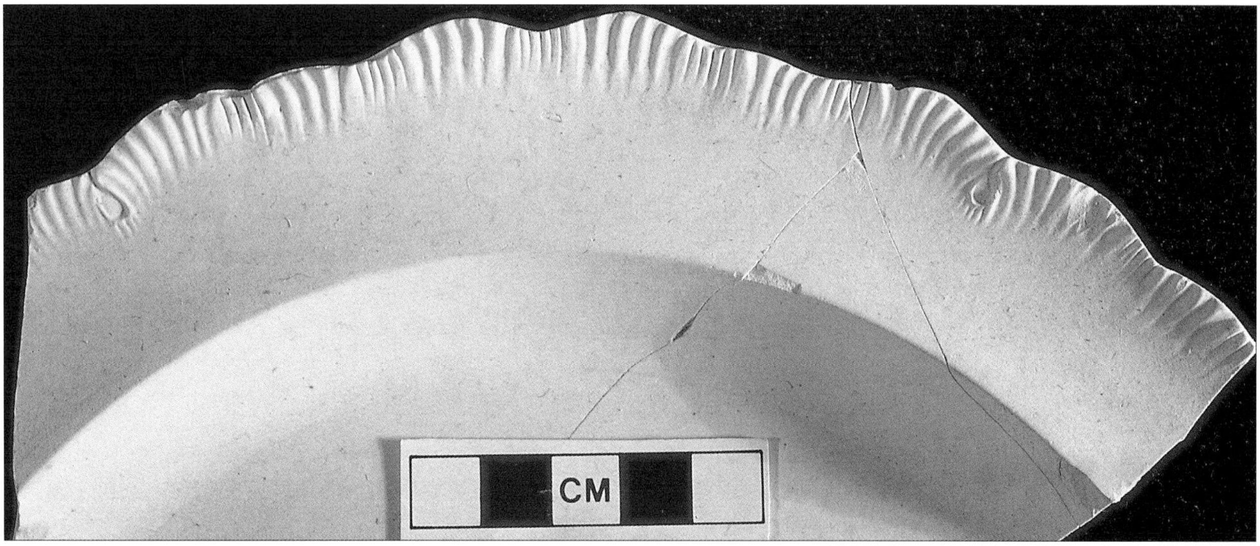

Fig.13x Dinner plate, 'Shell' border with wavy edge, Type A

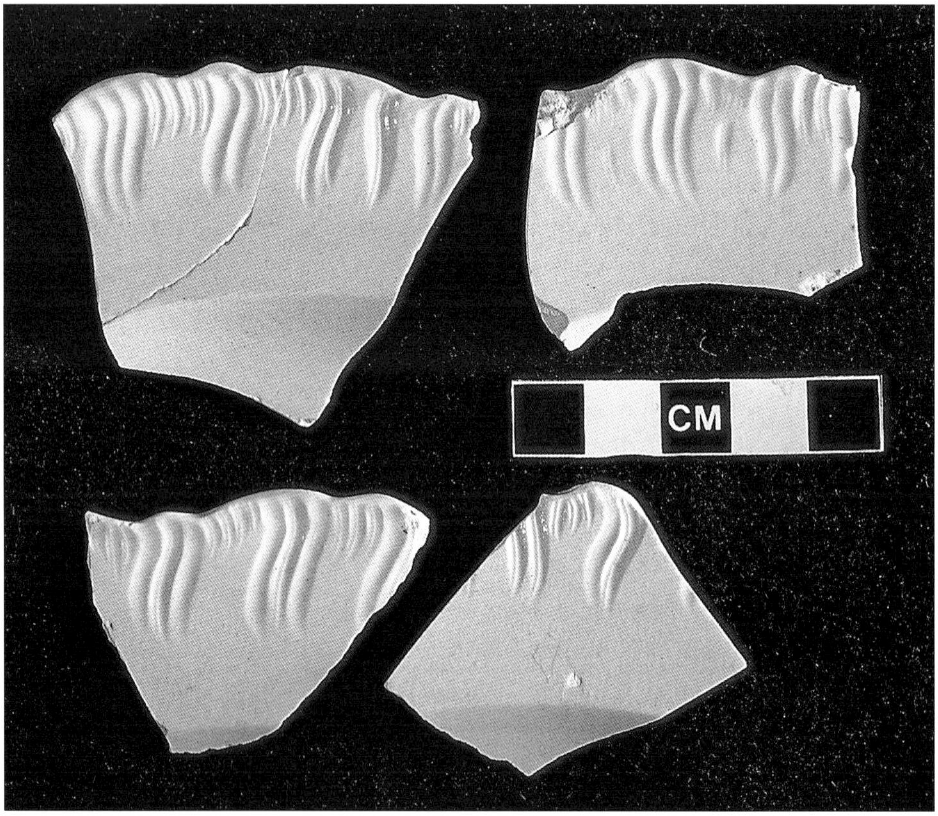

Fig.13xi Dinner plate fragments, 'Shell' border with wavy edge, Type B

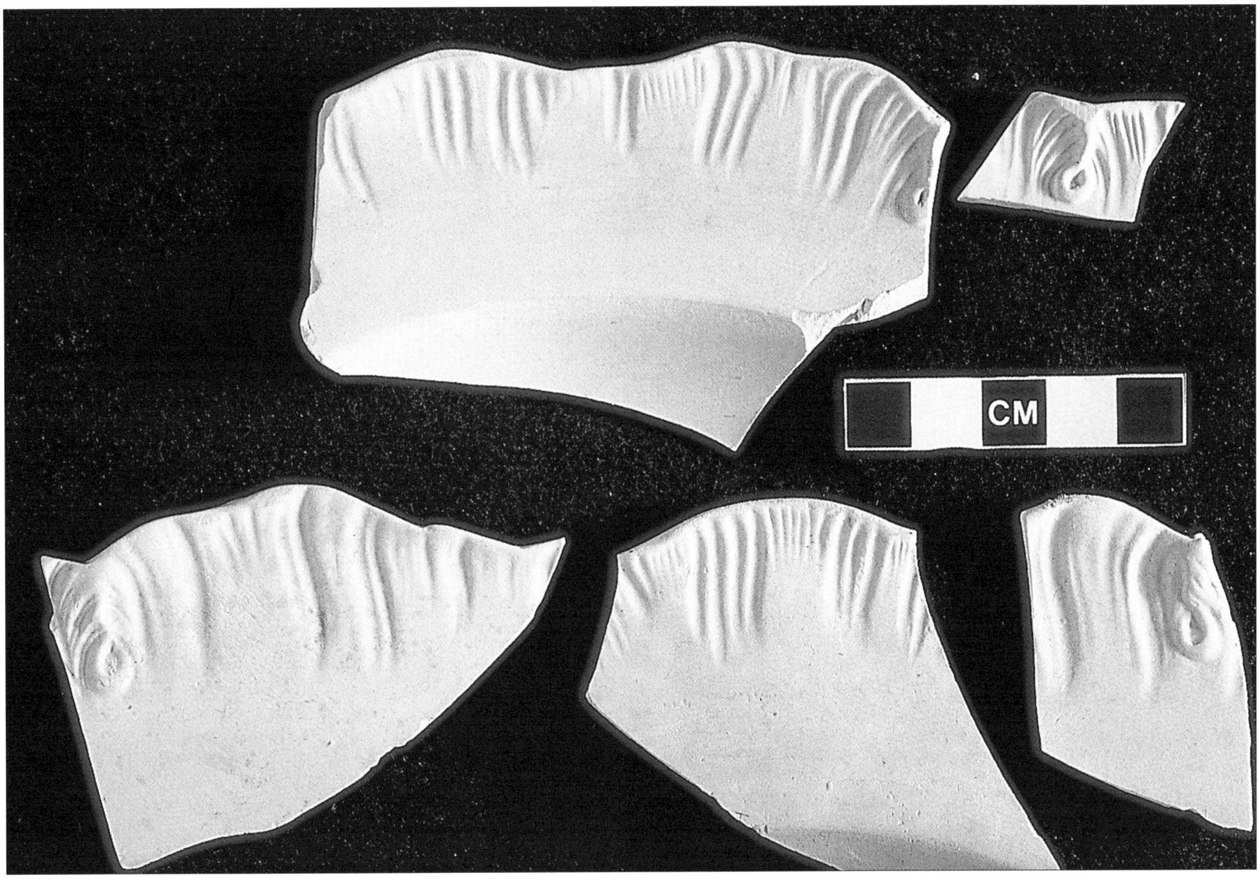

Fig.13xii 'Shell' border, wavy-edged platter fragments

Fig.13xiii Oval baking dish, 'Overlapped Shell' border, Type A

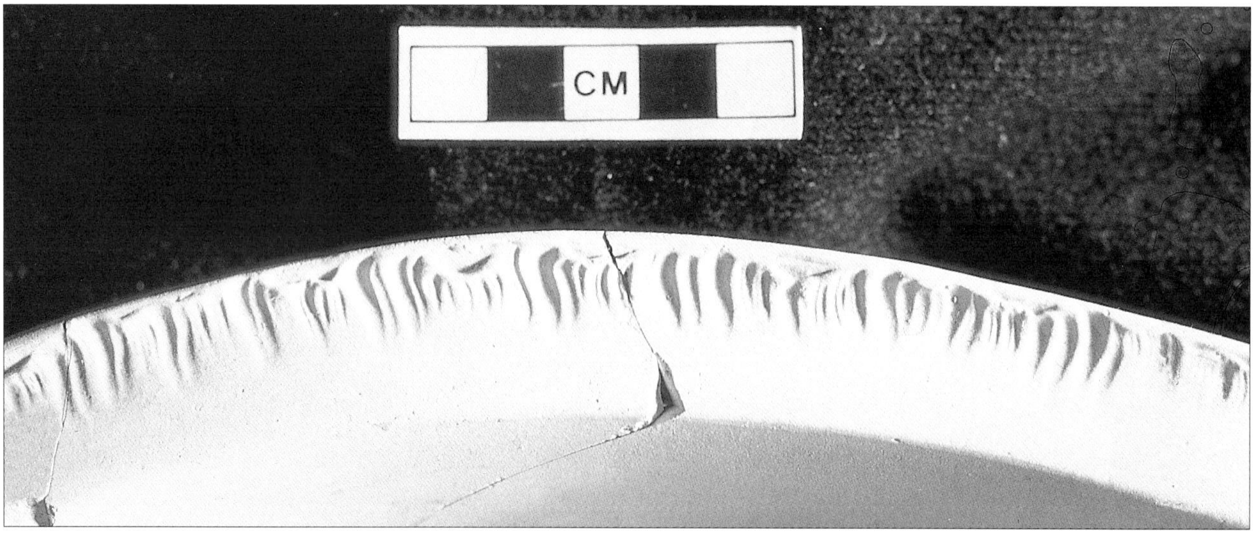

Fig.13xiv Detail of Fig. 13xiii

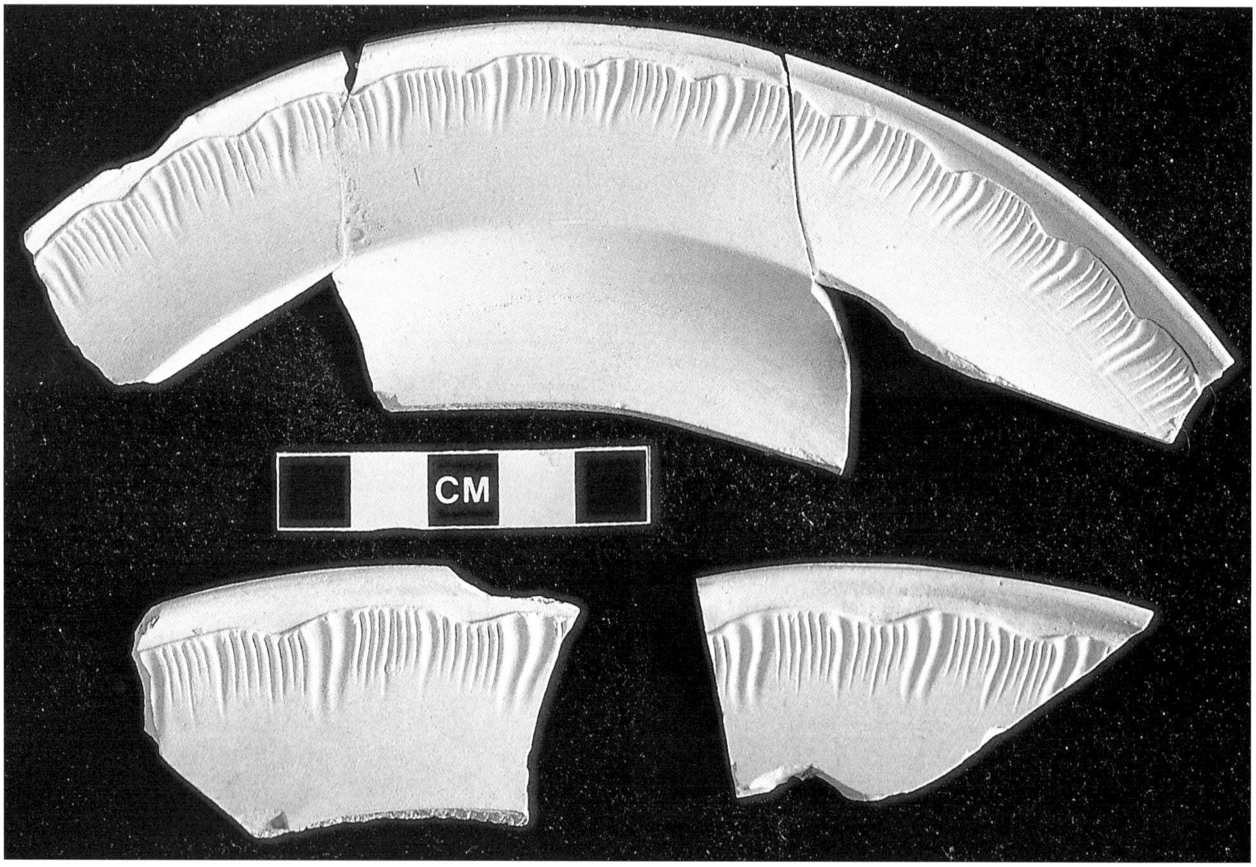

Fig.13xv Oval baking dish fragments, 'Overlapped Shell' border, Type B

14. SAUCE-BOATS (Figs. 14i–14vii)

Number of forms recorded:	5
Types of ware recorded:	Creamware
Height range:	70–75 mm
Footrim diameter range:	70–80 mm
Body decoration:	Various complex moulded decorative features (see illustrations)
Glaze decoration:	Plain, green 'shell' edge, yellow dot-moulded edge
Full profiles recorded:	2

A total of five different moulded sauce-boat forms were excavated. As the accompanying illustration from the Don Pottery catalogue indicates (14i), most competent creamware potteries of this period offered a comparable range of about half a dozen types of sauce-boat. In terms of attribution, the fact that all of the excavated forms had been manufactured by slip casting in plaster moulds should mean that all of the Downshire types are potentially 'diagnostic forms'. Whether the designs are sufficiently different from comparable English examples to be distinguishable, however, remains to be seen.

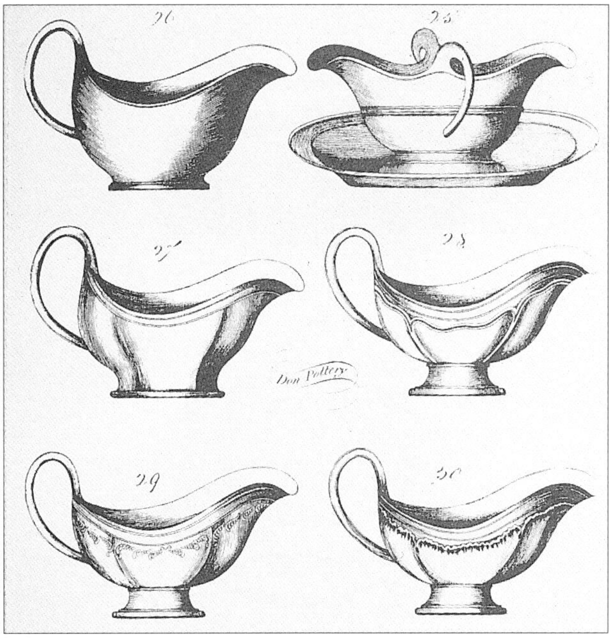

Fig.14i

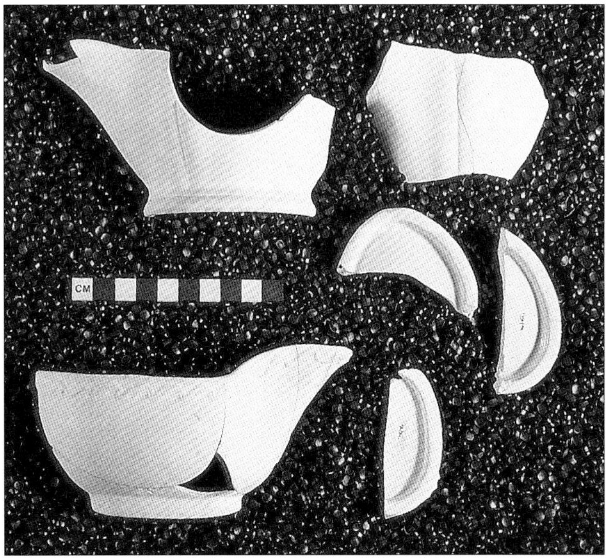

Fig.14ii

Type A 'Scalloped'

(14ii, upper four shards). Sufficient fragments of this pattern were found to allow a complete reconstruction of the form except for the handle. This is the plainest of the Downshire sauce-boats, and it most probably complemented the 'scalloped' plates that were also excavated (see Plates, Section 13, Figs. 13v–13vi). No decorated examples were found; all of the glazed fragments of this design appeared to be of plain creamware only.

Type B 'Leaf-edged'

(14ii, bottom row, 14iii, border motif, 14iv). This is among the most distinctive of all shapes excavated, especially as no examples of this type of 'leaf-edge' moulding appear to be recorded among comparable English pottery catalogues of the time. Sufficient fragments were recovered to allow the entire form to be reconstructed with the exception of the handle. Unfortunately, all of the shards recovered were of creamware biscuit rather than glazed, so that the style of glaze decoration is unknown.

Type C 'Shell-edged'

(14v. See also colour plate 7, top). No complete profiles of this type were found, although it seems clear from the style of the moulded border that this sauce-boat complemented the 'shell-edged' flatwares (See Plates, Section 13, types iv–vii, pp 58). Only one glazed and decorated example was found (top row, centre), on which the shell moulding has been highlighted in green. This design is also very similar to that which appears on one of the Downshire Pottery tureen fragments (Section 22, Fig. 22iii).

Type D 'acanthus-moulded'

(14vi). At first glance, this design appears similar to the 'shell-edged' type, but closer examination shows it to be a completely different form. Most shards of this pattern that were found came from close to the handle area, so that it was not possible to reconstruct a full profile, although the tall pedestal base is noteworthy. Glazed examples were of plain creamware, with no indication of painted decoration.

The existence of this particular design of sauce-boat improves the possibility that a much smaller but similar style of acanthus-moulded 'butter-boat' or 'pickle dish' could also have been made in Belfast (14vii). The Ulster

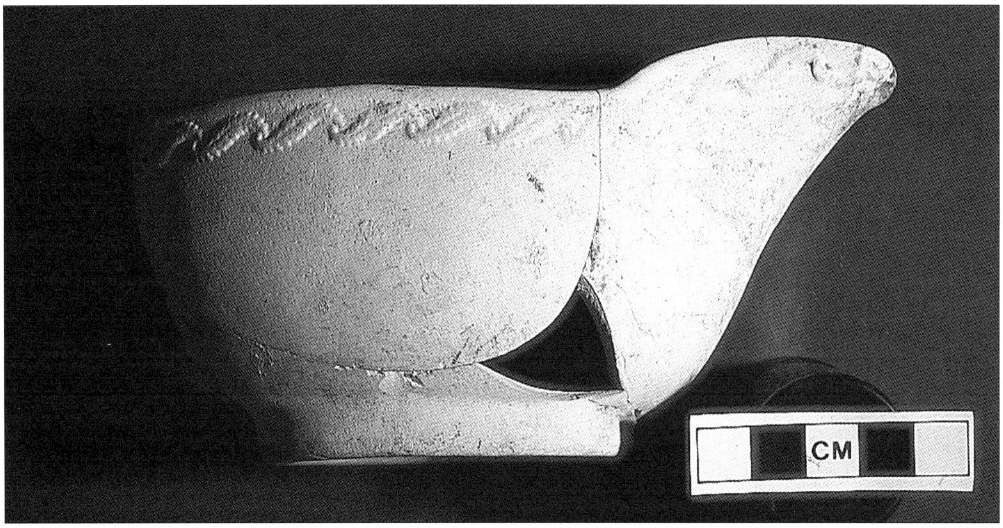

Fig.14iii

Fig.14iv

small dishes from the RM Young collection, attributed by Young to the Downshire Pottery. Unfortunately the shape – which derived from Meissen porcelain originally – was a very common one, and without tangible evidence from the excavation to confirm Young's speculation the attribution of these leaf dishes to Belfast must remain tentative.

Type E 'Yellow dot-moulded'

(14viii. See also colour plate 11, centre). This type of sauce-boat was represented by the single glazed and decorated shard illustrated. The bright yellow highlights on the dot-moulded band below the rim make this a most striking design, despite its simplicity.

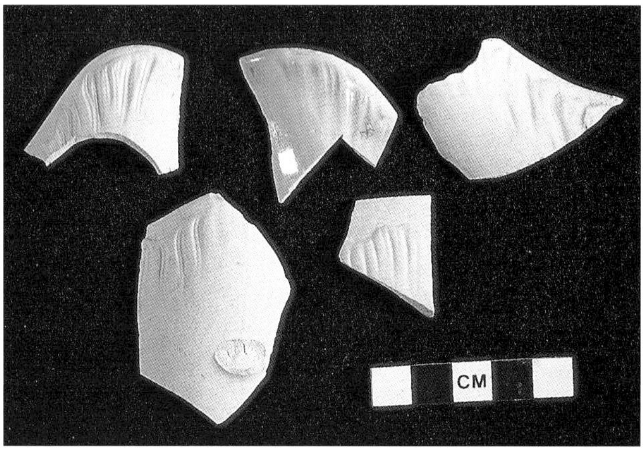

Fig.14v

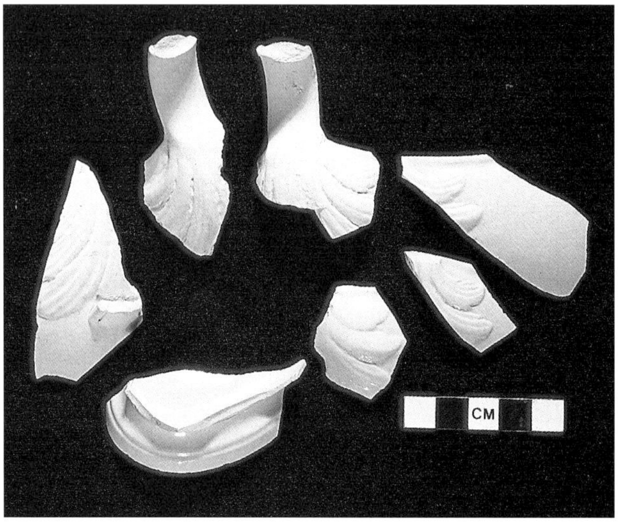

Fig.14vi

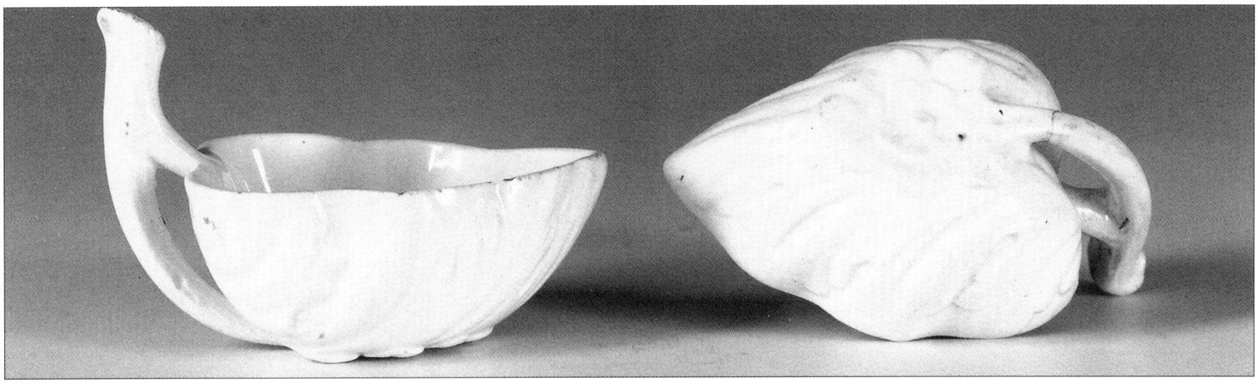

Fig.14vii

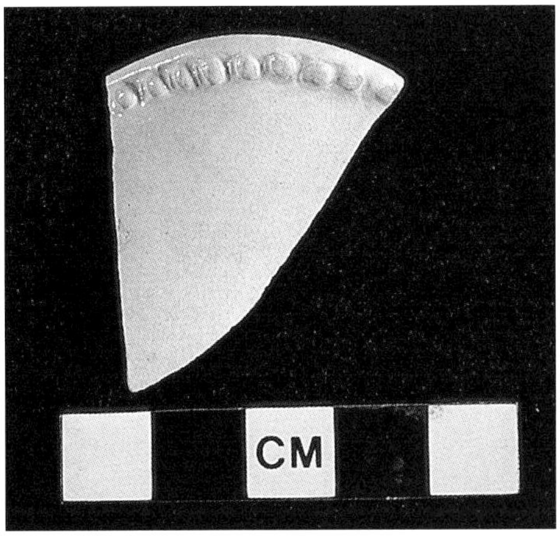

Fig.14viii

15. SAUCERS (Figs. 15i–15iii)

Catalogue numbers:	15/a/i–viii, 15/c/i and various decorated fragments
Types of ware recorded:	Creamware, pearlware
Rim diameter range:	120–160 mm
Footrim diameter range:	60–80 mm
Body decoration:	Plain, incised horizontal bands, machine-turned ribbing
Glaze decoration:	Floral and 'Chinese-style' painted, monochrome slip
Full profiles recorded:	> 6

The range of saucer fragments found was small and related directly to the equally restricted range of tea bowls (Section 18, p 66). Just two different saucer forms were observed:

Type A: Tall rounded saucer, with a wide rounded profile and high footrim (15i left and upper right).
Type B: Short, squat saucer with a more closely vertical profile and short footrim (15i centre).

Most of the saucer fragments found were entirely plain, but a small number of both types exhibited incised horizontal bands, sometimes incised through a monochrome slip (15i bottom right). Machine-turned examples were only found of type A, and even these were rare (15ii) although the illustration from the Don Pottery catalogue indicates that this was a comparatively standard design elsewhere. (15iii).

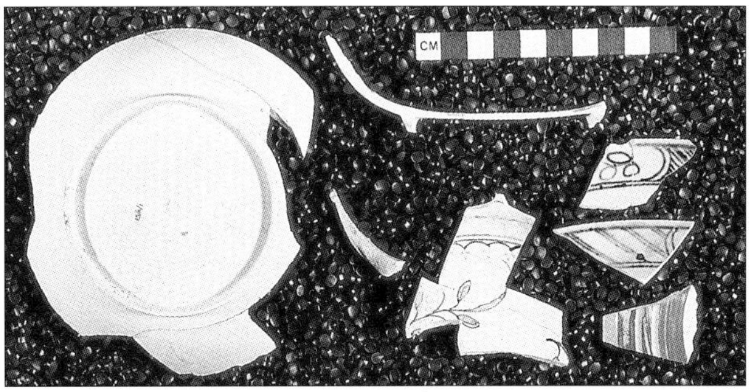

Fig.15i

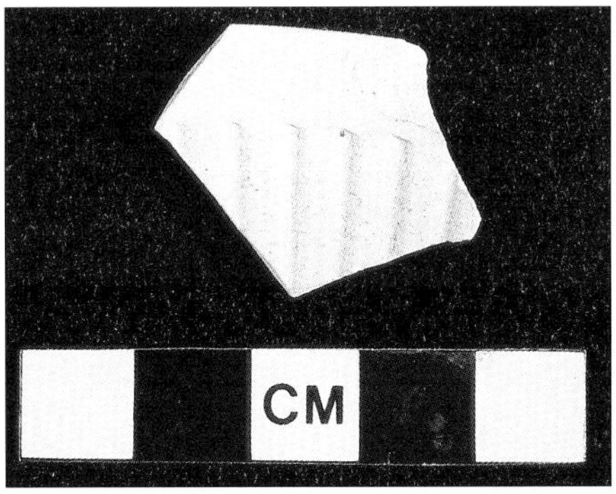

Fig.15ii

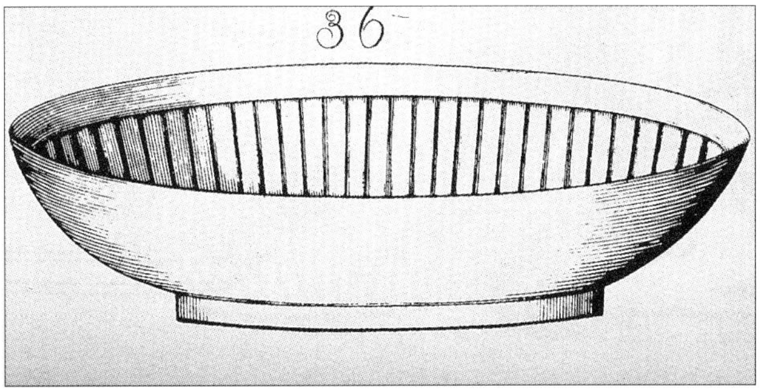

Fig.15iii

Although some otherwise unrecorded blue-painted pearlware borders were found (15i right), the most distinctive of the Downshire saucers found were those decorated with yellow, green and brown floral sprigs (15i lower right centre), which are very similar in appearance to floral sprigs on the reverse of the Downshire coffee-pot described previously.

16. STRAIGHT-SIDED VESSELS (Fig. 16i)

Number of forms recorded:	1 (of very variable dimensions)
Types of ware recorded:	Creamware, pearlware, fine and coarse buff-bodied ware
Height range:	72–90 mm
Rim and footrim diameter:	80–130 mm
Body decoration:	Plain, incised horizontal lines and bands
Glaze decoration:	Predominantly monochrome slip with incised plain lines
Full profiles recorded:	> 5

The general form of these straight-sided vessels can be readily seen in the illustration (16i), although their precise functions are not clear. There appear to be no signs of either handles or pouring lips, although the plain incised rim on some examples suggests that they probably possessed lids originally. They most likely were intended for use as simple storage canisters, of somewhat larger size overall than tea-canisters (Section 19).

Their comparatively simple decoration supports the notion that they were primarily functional objects, (none exhibited floral painting, for example). All of the creamware straight-sided vessels recorded were decorated with a monochrome slip and a few incised bands. Those made in buff-bodied ware were even more utilitarian in appearance, exhibiting only a few incised bands at most.

17. SUGAR BOWLS (Figs. 17i–17ii)

Number of forms recorded:	2
Types of ware recorded:	Creamware
Height:	Type i: approximately 100 mm, Type ii: 102 mm
Rim diameter:	Type i: not known, Type ii: 97 mm
Footrim diameter:	Type i: not known, Type ii: 82 mm
Body decoration:	(Both types) incised line, with floral sprig handle terminals
Glaze decoration:	(Both types) red-brown monochrome slip
Full profiles recorded:	Type i: none, Type ii: 1

The two vessels illustrated were among the more attractive and instructive wasters excavated (17i). (See also colour plate 2, left top and bottom). They have been interpreted as two different forms of sugar bowl, although it is possible that the second form (17i right) is simply a container of unspecific function. (It is identical to some of the straight-sided vessels described in Section 16 in all but its slightly more convex profile.)

The globular-bodied type A sugar bowl, (shown in 17i left and 17ii), is very finely made, with one floral-moulded handle termination remaining, (there would be four on an intact example), and the red-brown monochrome slip decoration bears a number of finely incised bands. There are no indications of handles on

Fig.16i

Fig.17i

the type B sugar bowl, (which also has a much straighter profile than type A).

The floral termination on type A is shown in detail in diagnostic features, p 77. In recent months, a powder-manganese sugar bowl and cover were found in an American collection, which bears floral-sprig handle terminations that are identical to those excavated in Belfast. There is a strong possibility therefore that this was produced at the Downshire Pottery (see colour plate 23).

18. TEA BOWLS

Types of ware recorded:	Creamware, pearlware
Height:	47–54 mm, average 50 mm
Rim diameter:	82–90 mm, average 85 mm
Footrim diameter:	37–50 mm, average 44 mm
Body decoration:	Plain, incised bands, machine-turned ribbing
Glaze decoration:	Underglaze painted, tortoiseshell
Full profiles recorded:	6

Only three, comparatively simple, tea bowl forms were recorded:

1. Plain (18i upper).
2. With incised horizontal bands (18i lower).
3. With vertical, engine-turned ribbing (18ii).

No complete profiles of the vertically-ribbed type were recorded, although a comparative illustration from the

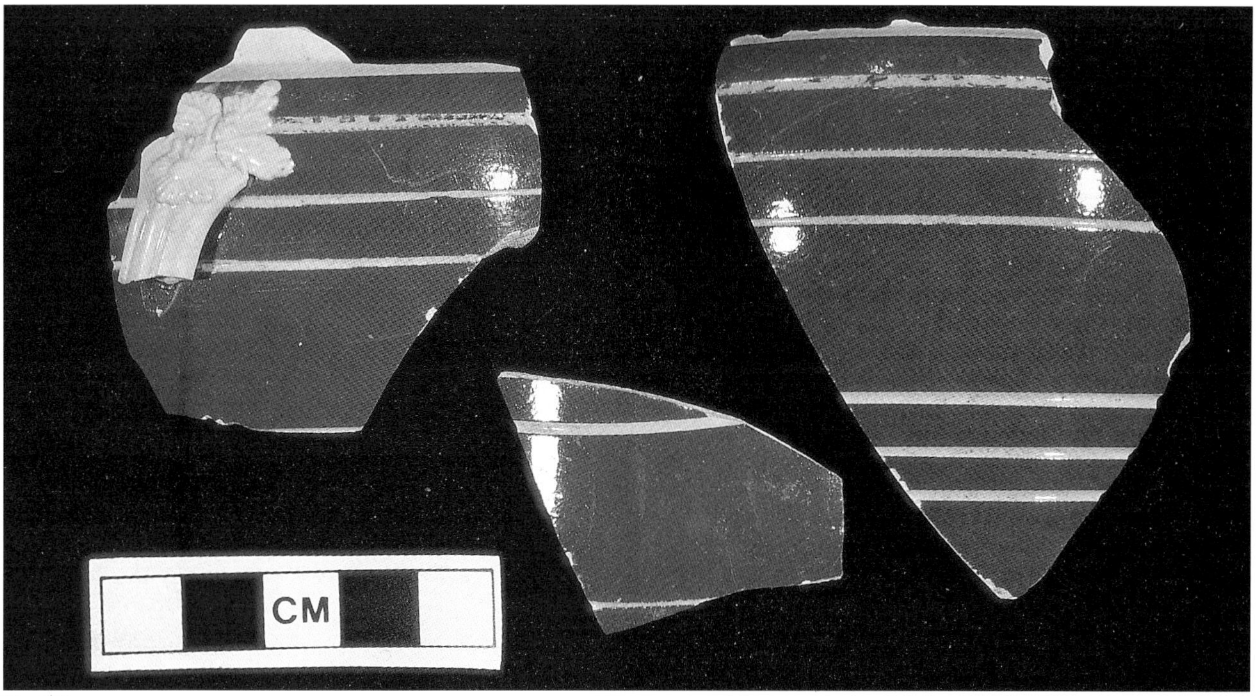

Fig.17ii

Fig.18i

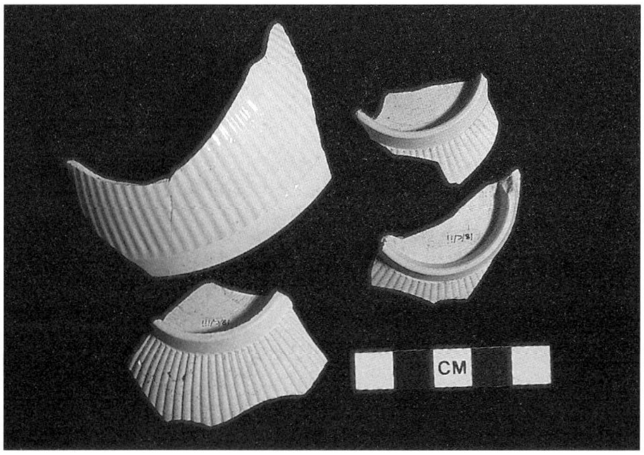

Fig.18ii

Don Pottery pattern book is of an identical form (18iii). As with the larger-sized bowls therefore (Section 3), there are no features among the Downshire tea bowl forms that can in any way be considered distinctive or diagnostic. The three designs match those already seen in the saucers (Section 15) and appear to have been the standard, basic types produced by a large number of potteries at that time.

Compared with the Don Pottery's modest output, we can see more clearly that the excavated assemblage from Belfast probably only represents a portion of what was actually made. For example, not one teacup was recovered, nor was there a coffee-can (comparable to the Don Pottery styles shown in 18iv). No tea bowls were found which bore shell-edge moulding, to complement the shell-edged flatwares that were recorded (Section 13). On balance, it seems entirely implausible that a pottery of this size and complexity did not make teacups, yet if we were to rely solely upon excavated objects then this would appear to be the case. It is easier to believe that the teacup wasters were simply dumped elsewhere.

Despite the restricted range of forms recovered, the styles of tea bowl decoration varied greatly. Painted designs were most common, (yellow, green and brown floral swags especially), but tortoiseshell and marbled-slip decorated examples were also present.

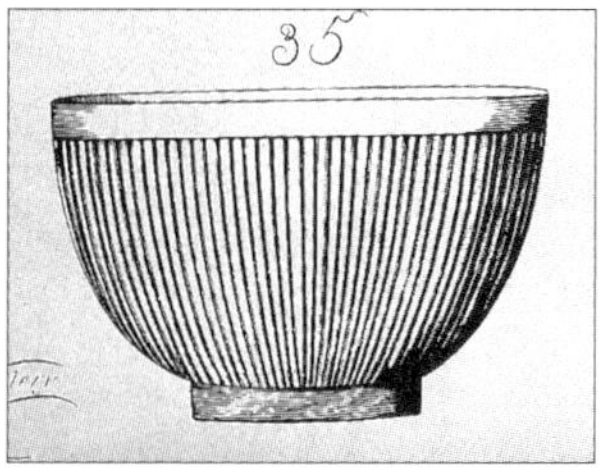

Fig.18iii

Fig.18iv

19. TEA CADDY OR CANISTER (Fig. 19i)

Types of ware recorded:	Creamware
Height:	Unknown
Rim diameter:	60 mm
Body decoration:	Unknown
Glaze decoration:	Overglaze enamel flower swag
Full profiles recorded:	None

A large number of fragments of straight-sided cylindrical vessels were recovered (see Section 16), many of which may have been tea-canisters fragments, but only one shard was positively identified as such (19i). The profile of this fragment is very similar to that of shards that have been classified as 'shouldered teapots' (Section 20), but on closer examination the canister shard is distinctly thinner (c.2 mm) and thus less capable of withstanding hot water.

It should be borne in mind therefore that some of the 'straight-sided vessel' or 'shouldered teapot' shards in the Downshire assemblage may, in fact, be fragments of tea-canisters. Otherwise it is difficult to understand why tea-canisters should have been quite so rare as this single shard would suggest.

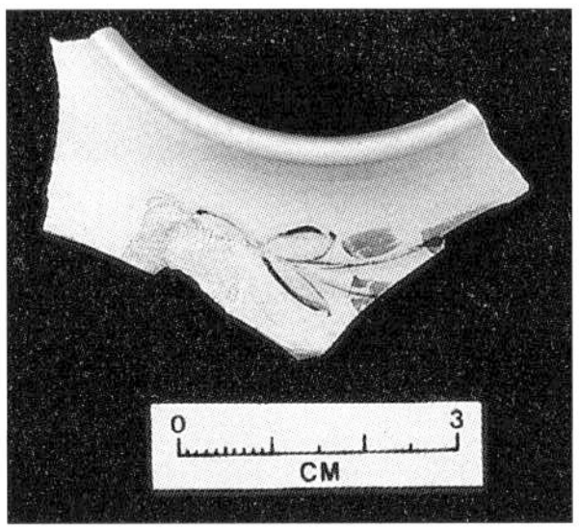

Fig.19i

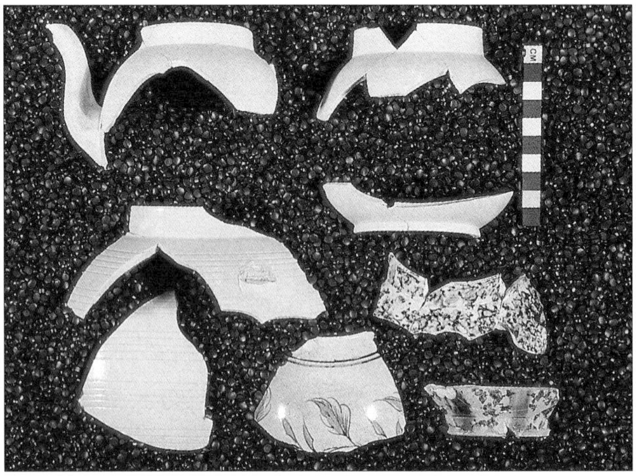

Fig.20i

Fig.20ii

20. TEAPOTS (Figs. 20i–20vi)

Number of forms recorded:	3
Types of ware recorded:	Creamware, pearlware
Body decoration:	Plain, incised horizontal lines and bands, some with moulded details
Glaze decoration:	Plain, monochrome slip, painted decoration, tortoiseshell
Full profiles recorded:	None

Three basic teapot forms were excavated:

Type A

Standard spherical teapot (Fig. 20i, top row). Estimated height range c.110–130 mm, average 125 mm, footrim diameter 60–75 mm, rim diameter 62–75 mm, rim height 10–13 mm.

Type B

Large spherical teapot (Fig. 20i, bottom left, with incised lines). Estimated height range c.180–200 mm, footrim diameter 100–130 mm, rim diameter c.100–130 mm, rim height 20 mm.

Type C

Straight-sided shouldered teapot (20iv). Estimated height range c. 120–180 mm, footrim diameter c. 70–120 mm, rim diameter 70–120 mm, rim height 15–25 mm (when present).

Two further teapot forms are attributed to the Downshire Pottery on the basis of their decoration, even though these forms were not excavated:

Type D

Globular teapot (Fig. 20ii, and colour plate 15).

Type E

Pedestal teapot (Figs. 20v and vi, see also colour plate 15) Footrim diameter 76 mm, lip diameter 76 mm, width of body 105 mm, height without lid 120 mm, height to top of handle 133 mm, height with lid 155 mm (knop restored).

The range of teapots excavated, like so much of the Downshire Pottery's range, were comparatively standard products in their time, and there are few distinctive characteristics to aid in identification of other examples. Some spherical teapots exhibited incised line decoration, but otherwise the most 'diagnostic' features on all teapots were their moulded spouts, handles and

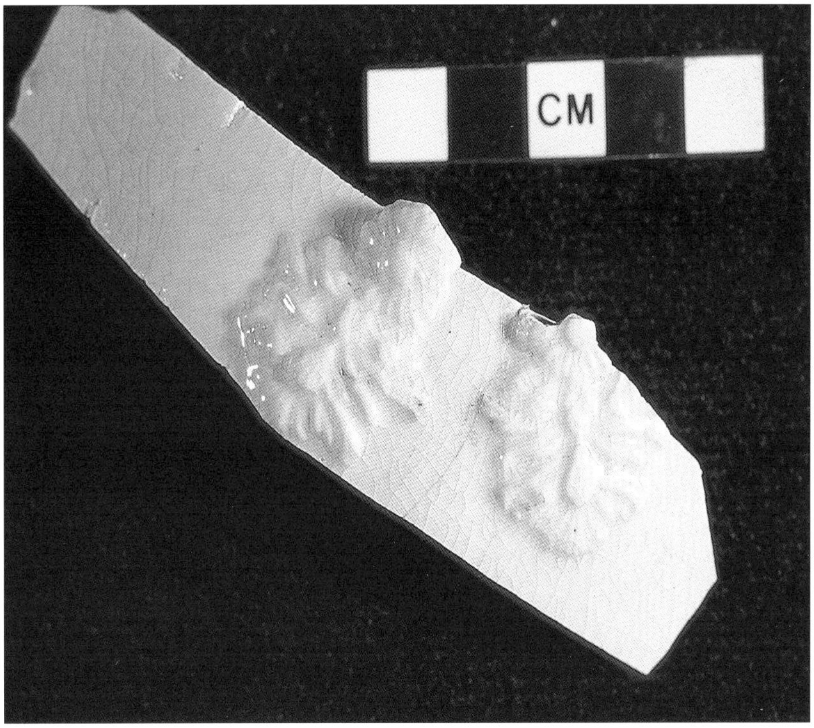

Fig.20iii

lids, described separately in diagnostic features, pp 73–79. As with Types D and E, Downshire Pottery teapots will probably be recognised in future on the basis of these diagnostic features – and by the style of decoration employed – rather than because the excavated forms are in any way distinctive.

A number of general observations are worth recording. The majority of Type A spherical teapots were decorated, and the quality of painted decoration was sometimes exceptionally good (see for example colour plate 10, top left). An unexpectedly large number of tortoiseshell decorated Type A teapot fragments were also recorded. In contrast, glazed fragments of the much larger Type B spherical teapot were entirely plain, with the exception perhaps of a few incised horizontal lines – presumably reflecting their more utilitarian character. Larger examples of the Type C straight-sided teapots were similarly plain and undecorated, but as only a small number of individual shards were excavated it is impossible to be more specific about the range of sizes that were produced.

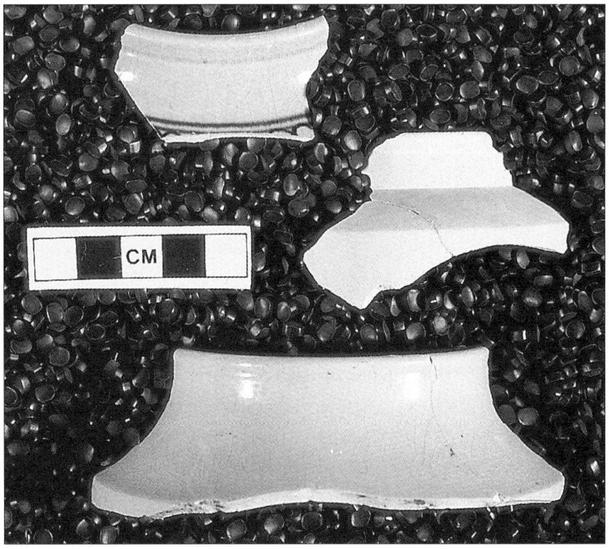

Fig.20iv

The Type D globular-bodied teapot, (20ii) in the author's collection, has primarily been attributed to Downshire on the basis of its moulded spout, supported by colour match to excavated tortoiseshell shards. A single shard was also excavated which matches the flat base and lower profile, suggesting that teapots of this approximate form were certainly produced, even if the precise profile and dimensions cannot be determined. Further evidence in support of this opinion derives from the plain white double handle terminations shown (20iii). Comparable examples of double-entwined handles on teapots are generally present on Type D teapots (with a completely rounded profile and recessed lid), rather than on Type A and B teapots (with a tall footrim and rim). These Type D teapots must have appeared old-fashioned in 1790 or 1791 when the Downshire Pottery commenced manufacture (comparable English examples are generally dated c.1765–80), which in turn might suggest that some of Downshire's block and moulds may have been bought in from an earlier English pottery.

The Type E pedestal teapot in the Ulster Museum collection (20v–20vi), is undoubtedly the most distinctive form that is presently attributed to the Downshire Pottery, principally on the basis of its moulded spout and the overglaze-enamelled decoration, which both match excavated examples. The complex moulded handle (see diagnostic features, p 79) is particularly distinctive, and similar to (but not identical to) handles produced by William Greatbatch in Staffordshire during the early 1780s (Greatbatch handle types 7 and 8).

The enamel decoration of the Downshire teapot is obviously unusual: while the flower garlands are adequately painted, the written text on each side is misspelt and poorly arranged. The religious reference 'No Cross No Crown' is clear, but the longer inscription 'My Grace is Suffitiant for the Annah Prince' should probably be interpreted as 'My Grace is Sufficient For Thee... Anna Prince'. (In other words, commissioned for Anna Prince.) It is known from documentary evidence that an overglaze enamel painter – Thomas Davis Bayley – was employed to work at the Downshire Pottery, and may have begun to train some apprentices in 1793, but difficulties were encountered in gaining his services later (see page 9). Perhaps the unusual enamelling on this teapot reflects some of these difficulties.

Fig.20v

Fig.20vi

21. TOY TEA-WARES (Fig. 21i)

Number of forms recorded:	3 (tea bowl, sparrowbeak jug and 'sugar bowl') (?)
Types of ware recorded:	Creamware biscuit
Height:	Tea bowl c. 25 mm, sparrowbeak jug c. 50 mm (estimated)
Rim diameter:	Sparrowbeak jug 20 mm, tea bowl rim not recorded
Footrim diameter:	Tea bowl 15–16 mm, jug 22 mm, 'sugar bowl' (?) 12 mm
Body decoration:	Plain forms only
Glaze decoration:	No glazed examples recorded
Full profiles recorded:	None

Fragments of three types of these exceptionally small tea-wares were found:

1. Miniature tea bowls, with footrim diameters of 15–16mm, (5/8 inch), and an estimated height of about one inch.
2. Miniature sparrowbeak jugs, with rim diameters of approximately 20 mm (3/4 inch), and an estimated height of about two inches.
3. Miniature flat-based vessel, with an exceptionally small footrim diameter (12 mm), of unknown form.

The miniature sparrowbeak jug and tea bowl shards have been illustrated alongside their full-sized equivalents to emphasise their exceptionally small size (Fig. 21i). The forms of these toy tea-wares are entirely plain, with no moulded details or distinctive features to aid identification. No glazed examples were found, and so the styles of decoration are also unknown.

Comparable miniature teasets were produced by many of the Staffordshire potters, notably Wedgwood, presumably for children or dolls' houses. As with the full-sized teasets which they imitated, many were plain, others bore complex decoration. Complete sets which have survived typically include a serving-tray, coffee-pot,

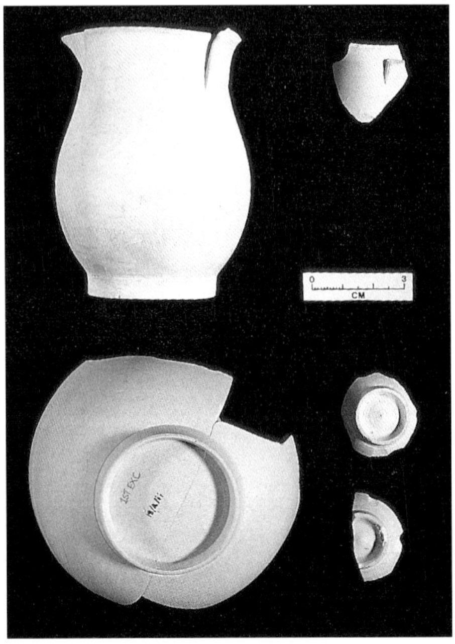
Fig.21i

teapot, kettle, tea-canister, sparrowbeak jug, covered slop-bowl and sugar bowl, together with four or six tea bowls, teacups and saucers.

22. TUREENS (Figs. 22i–22iii)

Number of forms recorded:	4 (2 small, 2 large)
Types of ware recorded:	Creamware
Body decoration:	Plain, 'shell-edged'
Glaze decoration:	Plain, green shell-edge, tortoiseshell, (see tureen lids)
Full profiles recorded:	2

Two basic types of tureen body were recorded: plain (small, large oval and large circular) and shell-edged (small), but this is certainly just a small portion of the range of tureens that were actually produced. Among the tureen lids, for example, (see diagnostic features, pp 79–80) are several designs which were not recorded among the tureen body fragments. The border designs of some of the sauce-boats (Section 14) also indicate that other types of tureen were probably produced by the Downshire Pottery, but were not found during the excavations, (Sauce-boat types ii and v for example).

Comparatively few tureen body fragments were recognised, so that the recorded dimensions are correspondingly scant.

Type i: Plain oval, small (22i, top right).
Type ii: Plain oval, large (22i, centre and bottom right).
Type iii: Plain oval, circular (22i, bottom left). Only one footrim fragment of this type was recorded, with a footrim diameter of 133 mm. The height of the pedestal base is also lower than the Type ii tureen. (The two types are shown side by side, 22i bottom left and right.)
Type iv: 'Shell-edge', small (22i, top left, and Fig. 22iii. See also colour plate 7, top). All of the fragments recovered of this design were parts of a single glazed example, with a green-painted shell moulding.

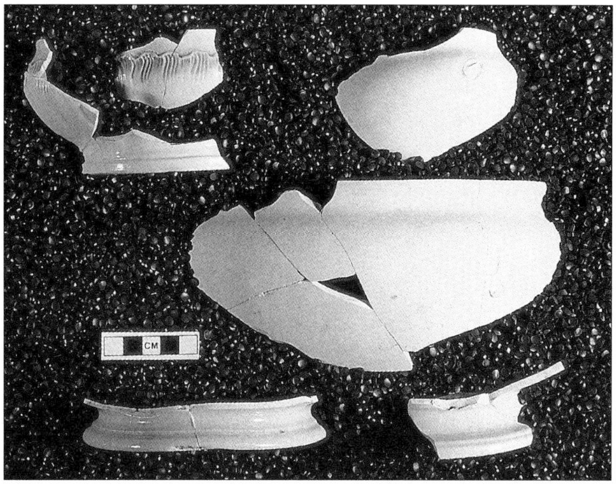

Fig.22i

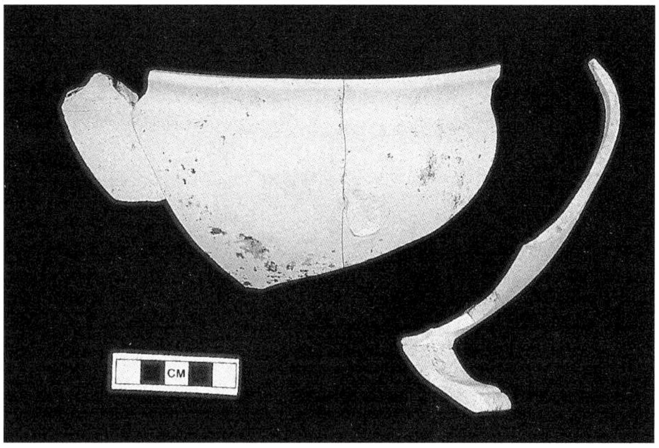

Fig.22ii

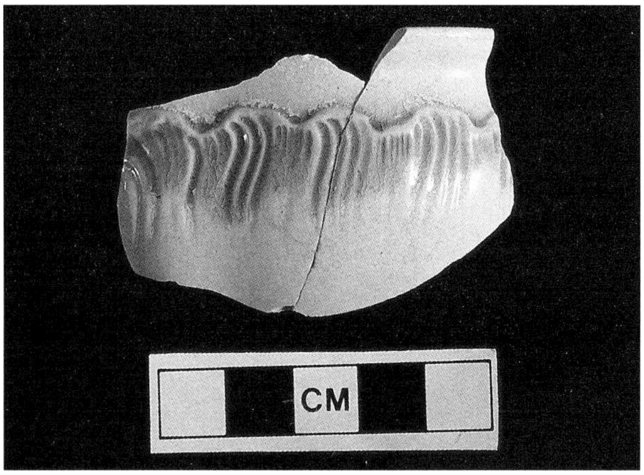

Fig.22iii

23. VINTNER'S BIN LABEL (Figs. 23i–23ii)

Number of forms recorded:	1
Types of ware recorded:	Creamware biscuit
Height:	75 mm
Width:	115 mm
Thickness:	4 mm
Glaze decoration:	No glazed fragments recorded
Full profiles recorded:	1

This single, intact ceramic wine bin label was one of the more unexpected objects to be excavated. Despite appearing to be in perfect condition, (23i) it was probably discarded because the hole on the topmost point (from which the label would have been suspended) was not fully pierced. Comparable ceramic bin labels produced elsewhere were usually glazed, and they frequently bear the names of a wide variety of alcoholic drinks, mainly wines (either enamelled or transfer-printed). Others were sold in the unglazed biscuit state rather than glazed, so that individual vintners could record the wine's details on such labels in pencil.

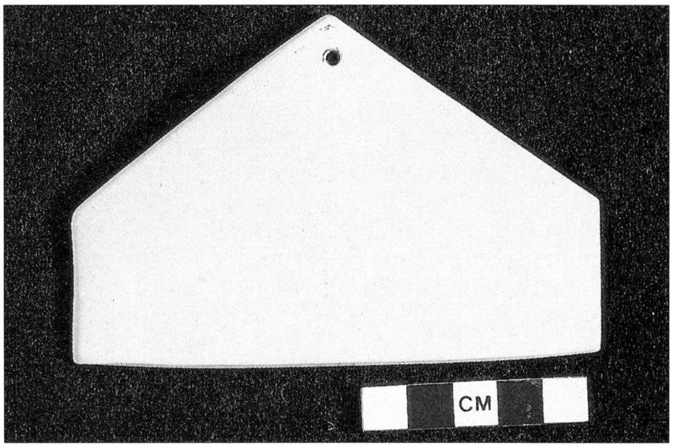

Fig.23i

Despite its apparent simplicity the bin label was formed in a plaster mould (rather than cut to shape from a clay sheet), which is useful for attribution purposes, for it means that there is a strong possibility that any bin label of *precisely* identical size and shape is a Downshire product (23ii).

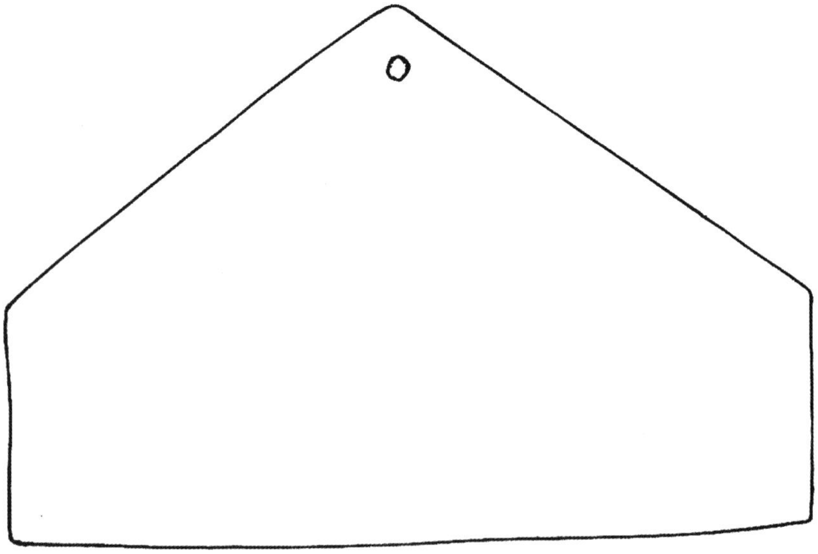

Fig.23ii Actual size of Downshire bin label

24. DIAGNOSTIC FEATURES (Figs. 24i–24xxviii)

The term 'diagnostic features' embraces a wide variety of small features such as handles, spouts and lids, rather than a specific group of complete objects. When attempting to identify the origins of almost any piece of unmarked creamware, the smallest details are often the most useful. In theory at least, each of the different 18th-century creamware potteries, whether Wedgwood, Leeds, Belfast or elsewhere, manufactured such details using their own, factory-specific moulds. Consequently, it *should* be possible to recognise the wares of any individual pottery by the small differences which exist among these moulded details, even though the output of many creamware potteries was exceptionally similar in general terms.

This attractive theory was certainly popular in the early days of creamware research, but sadly it has not held up to scrutiny. The master moulds (from which plaster of Paris moulds were taken) were produced by highly skilled modellers, and recent research suggests that many creamware potteries simply bought-in their master moulds or plaster copies as required, rather than retaining the services of a full-time modeller. Further work is required to fully resolve these speculations, but it is certainly known already that at least four potteries in Stoke-on-Trent shared moulds, and it would be surprising to find that the practice was not very much more widespread than was previously recognised.

It is difficult, therefore, to assess the 'uniqueness' of any of the moulded details that appear on the Downshire Pottery's wasters. The documentary evidence suggests that Downshire was unable to use English materials in manufacturing its wares, and if this is accurate then the various mouldings should, in theory, be reasonably distinctive. Countering this argument, however, are the wares themselves, which often seem so very similar to comparable English wares as to be indistinguishable, suggesting that there must have been a comparatively free flow of skilled workmen and materials across the Irish Sea, despite the written evidence. One possibility, suggested by the old-fashioned style of some Downshire products (certain teapots for example, Section 20), is that some of their moulds were bought in as 'old stock', or perhaps came from an English pottery that had closed down. Without further evidence, the possibilities for speculation are endless.

Even if it transpires that the Downshire mouldings are genuinely 'diagnostic', the range of such features was small when compared to those of many potteries in Britain, perhaps reflecting the fact that all of the excavated wares recovered were produced during the Downshire Pottery's first year or two of production. Nonetheless, and bearing all of these negative observations in mind, there are certainly reasons for believing that the Downshire Pottery exhibited some degree of consistency in the range of handles, spouts and so on that it made, in which case it is hoped that these detailed photographs will ultimately prove useful.

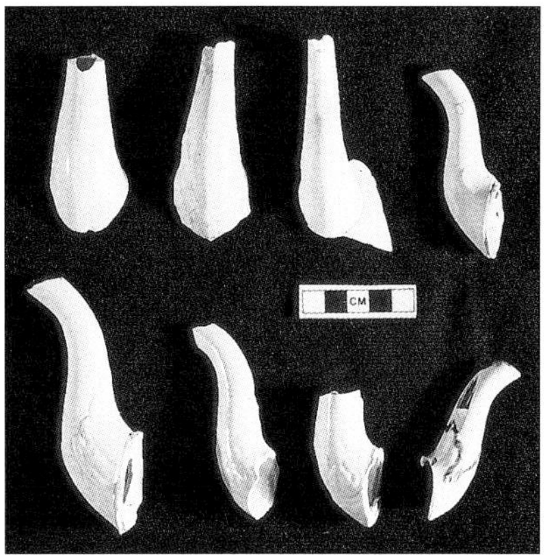

Fig.24i

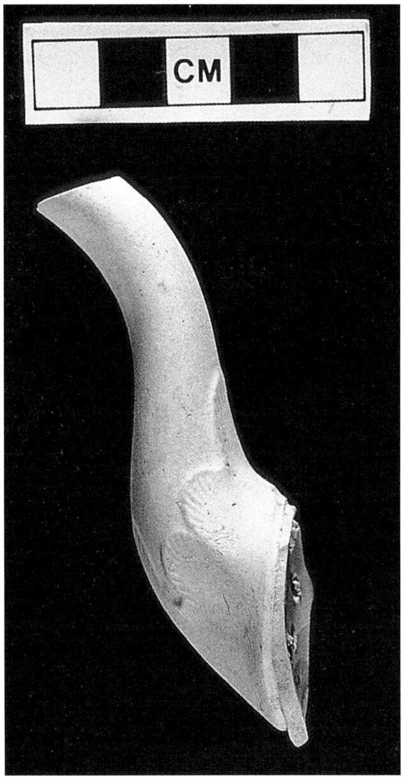

Fig.24ii

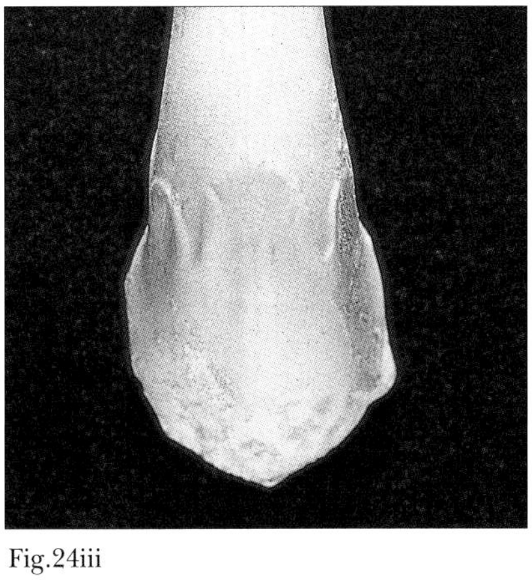
Fig.24iii

24a. Spouts

Four basic designs of tea and coffee-pot spouts were found, one of them in two sizes.

i. Plain (basal width 35 mm).
ii. Feather-moulded with plain edge (basal width 30 mm).
iii. Feather-moulded with serrated edge (basal width 32 mm).
iv. Acanthus-moulded
  – small (basal width 29 mm).
  – large (basal width 41 mm).

1. Teapot and coffee-pot spouts (Figs. 24i–24vi)

Illustrations:

24i: shows the relative sizes of all five types. (Top row, left to right: plain and feather-moulded forms. Bottom row: large and small acanthus-moulded forms. The pearlware example, bottom right, has been highlighted in underglaze blue.)

24ii: close-up view of Type iii (feather-moulded), showing the small, moulded 'serrations' around the margins of the 'feathers'. (Type ii is identical but without these serrations.)

24iii: front view of the Type iii spout shown in 24ii.

24iv: details of the small and large versions of the Type iv spout (acanthus-moulded).

24v: detail of the tortoiseshell-decorated teapot illustrated in colour plate 15, left, attributed to the Downshire Pottery, showing the small acanthus-moulded spout, (Type iv).

24vi: close-up view of the large Type iv, acanthus-moulded spout. The large size and vertical aspect of this spout suggest that it was more likely used on coffee-pots, rather than on large teapots.

2. Jug and other spouts (Figs. 24vii–24ix)

Just one form of moulded jug spout was recorded amongst the excavated wasters – the acanthus-moulded spout shown in 24, vii, (which presumably complemented the acanthus-moulded tea and coffee-pot spouts).

A second, larger form of acanthus-moulding is evident on the large, barrel-shaped jug (24viii), also shown in colour plate 13, which is *attributed* to the Downshire Pottery (see page 30).

It is also possible that the small fragment recorded bearing a yellow-highlighted dot pattern border, (24ix left) may have come from a broad-spouted, helmet-shaped jug (similar in form to the small jug shown in colour plate 17). The style of painted border decoration which occurs on the jug-spout shown overleaf, (24ix, right), is also distinctive, and should be readily recognisable on an intact example.

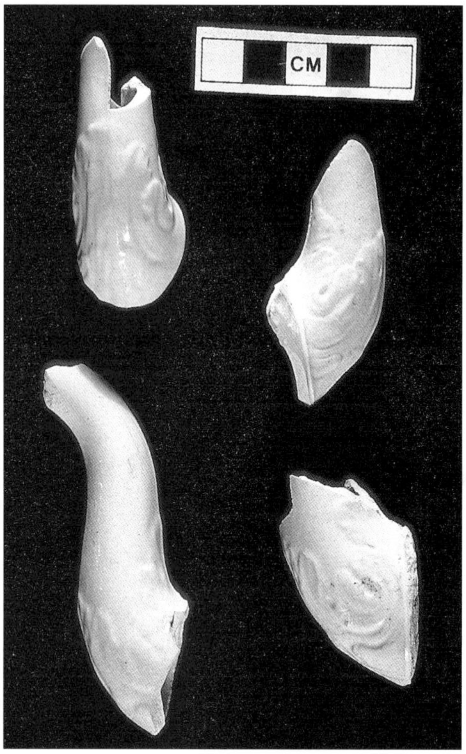

Fig.24iv

Fig.24v

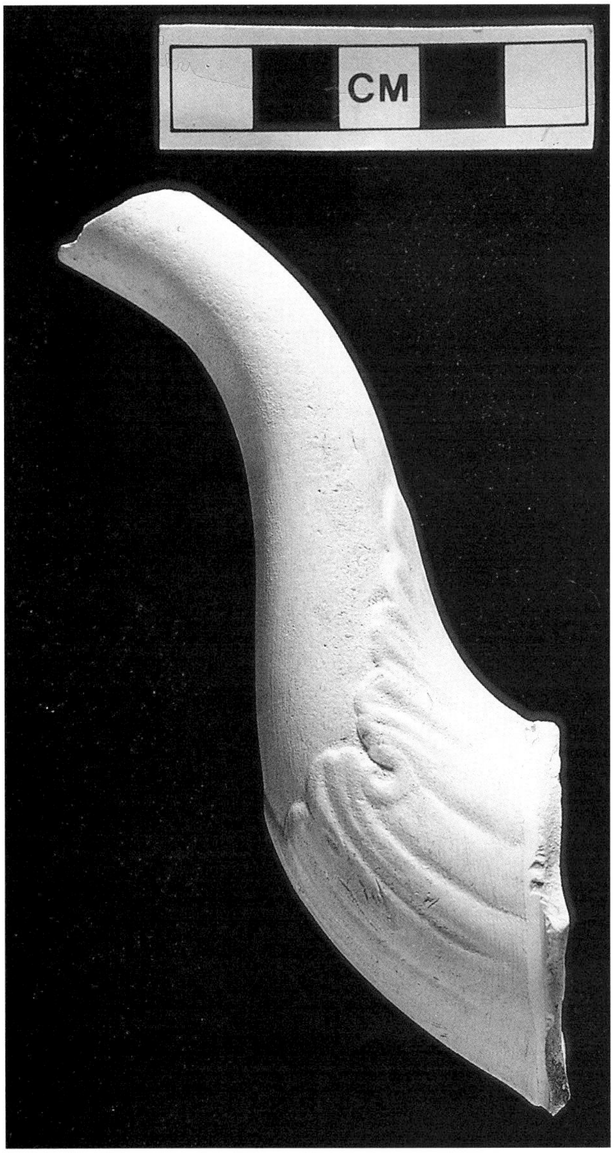

Fig.24vi

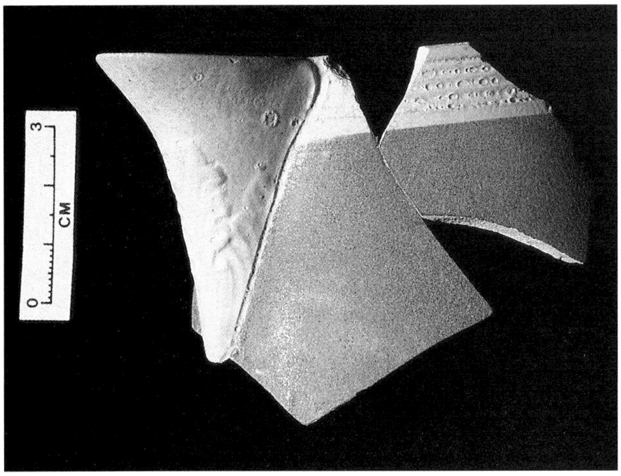

Fig.24vii

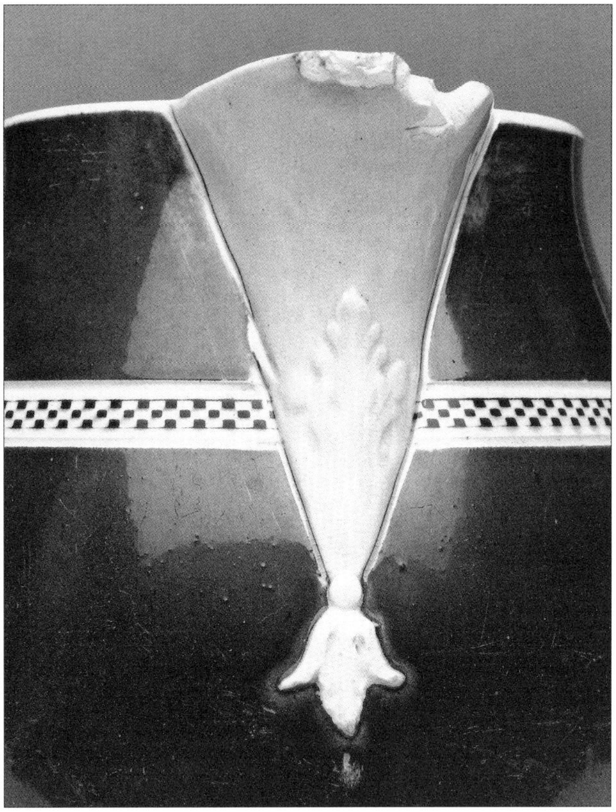

Fig.24viii

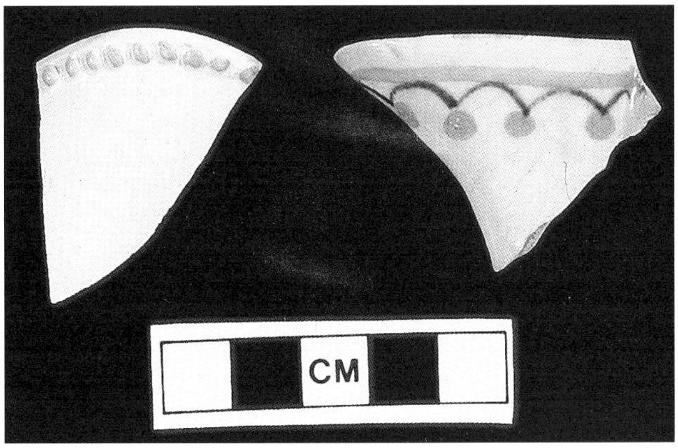

Fig.24ix

24b. Handles (Figs. 24x–23xxii)

1.Plain (strap) handles (Figs. 24x–24xii)

The majority of handles recovered were of very simple form (24x, top row) – usually just plain strap handles, sometimes finished with an indented edge on each side (24x, top right).

A number of plain strap handles were also excavated which bore secondary, underglaze-painted decoration (24xi). A total of six, fairly rudimentary, designs were found; some in cobalt blue (nos 1–3), others in manganese brown (nos 4–6), although no 5 is painted in a brown-green combination.

The painted handle design which appears on the large Ulster Museum jug (colour plate 21) was not recorded on the excavations (24xii), but it bears strong similarity to the excavated handle design No. 6. This also appears on the attributed coffee-pot (shown in colour plate 20).

2.Braided handles and terminals (Figs. 24xiii–24xvii)

Two examples were found of this complex handle, (24xiii), formed by loosely braiding two shaped, extruded lengths of clay. (The clay lengths were later dipped in lead glaze and hence fused on firing.)

At first sight, these highly decorative handles appear to have come from a lightweight article – a basket perhaps, but closer examination of comparative material suggests that they almost certainly come from a globular-bodied teapot. A pair of related handle terminals appear to have come from a similar teapot – they may even be part of the same object (24xiv). Obviously, there is a possibility that these terminals may prove diagnostic; the details are more easily recognised in the accompanying line drawings. (A noticeable characteristic is the presence of one long frond on the right hand side of the moulding – indicated with an arrow.)

A second type of flower terminal was also recorded (24xvi and xvii), on a sugar bowl and on a tankard fragment. Once again, the flower appears to be a terminal for a double-entwined or braided handle rather than for a standard strap handle. A particular feature to note in this moulding is a small, heart-shaped detail just below the flower (see arrow, 24xvii). This feature is present on the sugar bowl recently discovered in a private American collection (colour plate 23).

3.Moulded handles (Figs. 24xviii–24xxii)

Only two moulded handle forms were found by the excavation. The first (24xviii) is part of a pearlware double-handle, enhanced with underglaze blue decoration on the outside edge. The second is the basal portion of a copper-green painted, 'acanthus-moulded' large jug handle (24xix).

The form of this latter handle is similar to, but smaller than, the handle of the brown jug illustrated in colour plate 13, which is *attributed* to the Downshire Pottery (24xx).

Finally, the two illustrations of the highly unusual basket-woven handle which appears on the Ulster Museum teapot (colour plate 15, right), which is also *attributed* to the Downshire Pottery has been included (24xxi–xxii). The form of this handle is very similar to, but not identical to, a handle form that was excavated on the site of William Greatbatch's pottery (Barker, Fig. 27, Type B).

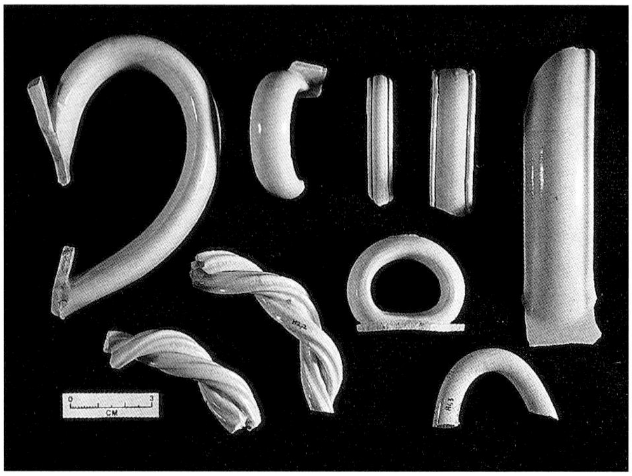

Fig.24x

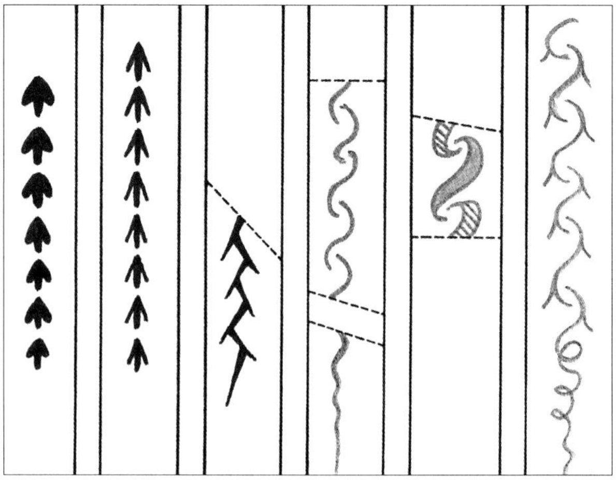

Fig.24xi

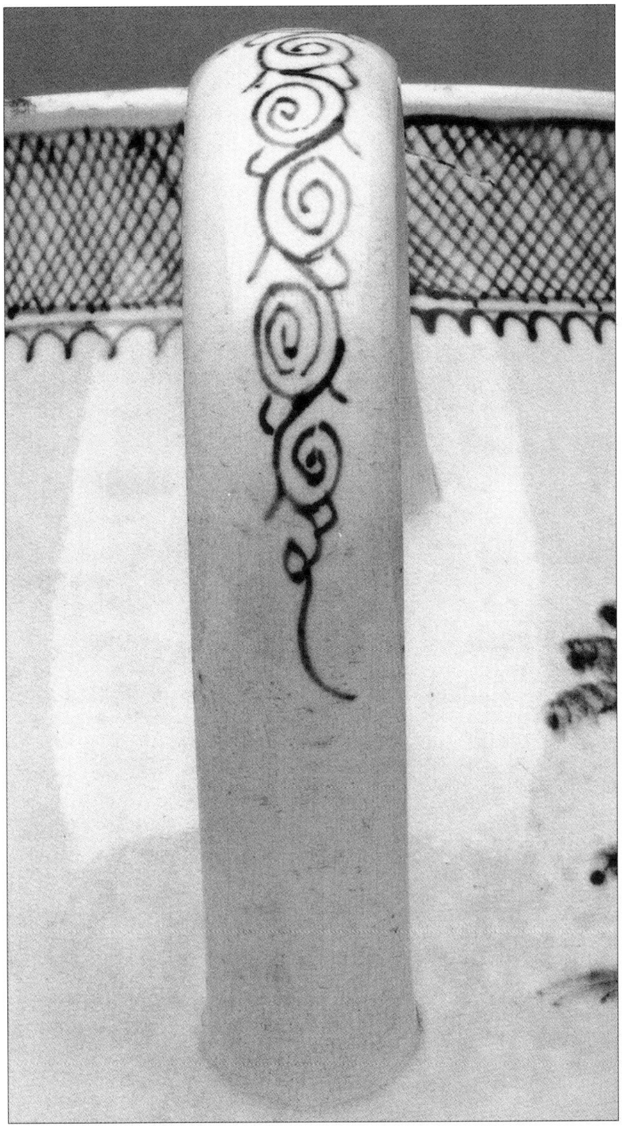

Fig.24xii

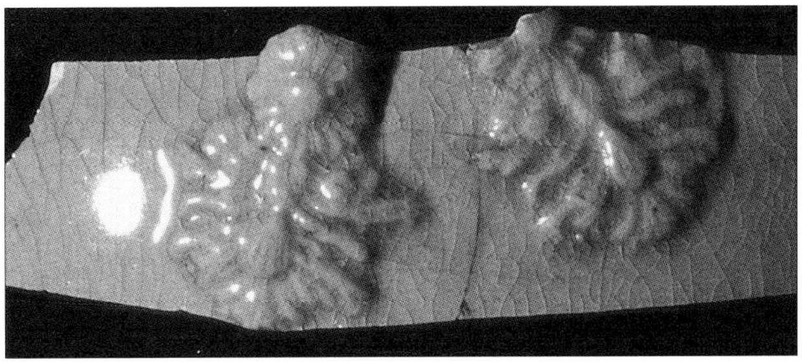

Fig.24xiv

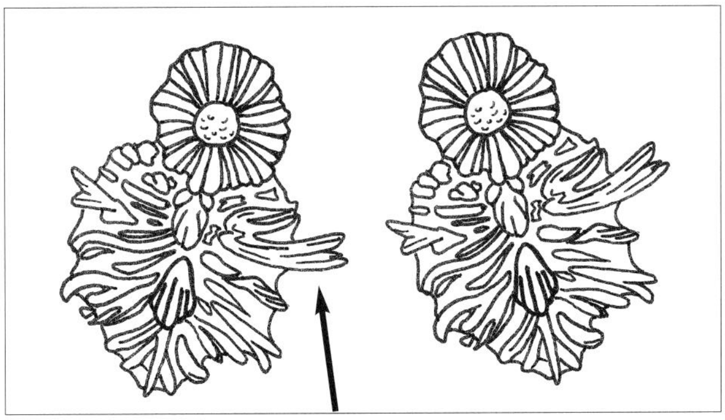

Fig.24xv

Fig.24xvi

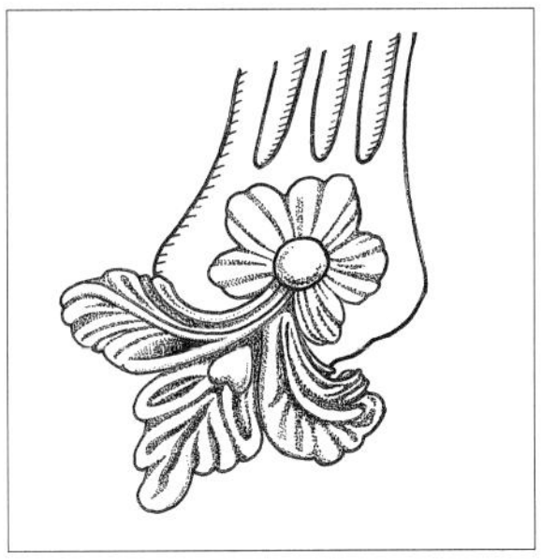

Fig.24xvii

Fig.24xiii

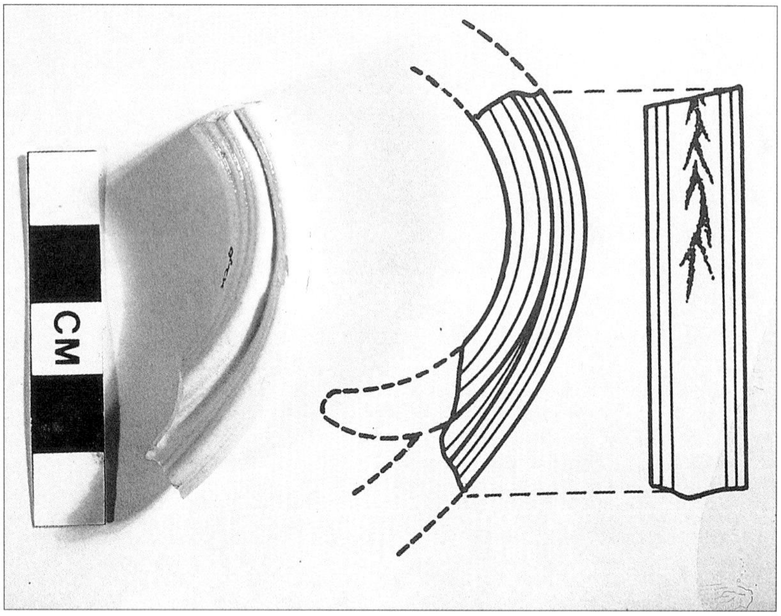

Fig.24xviii

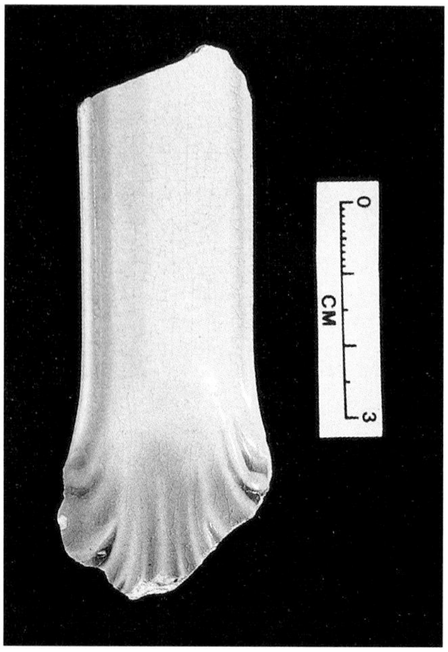

Fig.24xix

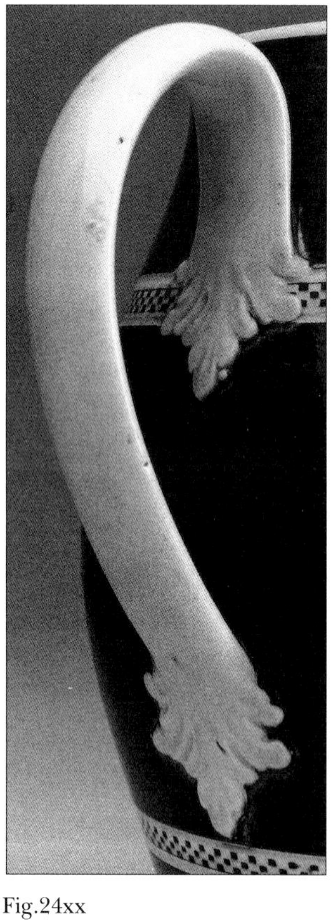

Fig.24xx

Fig.24xxi

Fig.24xxii

24c. Lids and Knops (Figs. 24xxiii–24xxviii)

1.Teapot, coffee-pot and small lids (Figs. 24xxiii–24xxiv) As can be seen in 24xxiii, most of the excavated lid-forms are comparatively plain and undiagnostic – decoration being limited to incised concentric lines (centre), or occasional radial engine-turning (top right).

The knops also are of simple form (24xxiv, left to right); either a simple, spherical shape, or, more usually, tear or drop shaped, sometimes on a small shaped step or 'plinth'. (See also 24xxiii, bottom left.)

2. Tureen lids and knops (Figs. 24xxv–24xxviii)

The range of tureen lids was larger than expected, for in addition to a plain lid (not illustrated), three complex moulded patterns were found. Only one of these three types (with acanthus-moulding) could be directly related to the designs of dinner-service recorded among the dinner-plates.

24xxv: Three fragments of an identical design of small tureen lid with radial, petal-like moulding. Examples were recovered in plain creamware (right) and with brown-tortoiseshell decoration. The design appears to be associated with two simple types of loop handle (extreme right).

24xxvi: Four biscuit-ware tureen lid fragments, of two designs. The top two fragments are of a radially-moulded 'silver-shaped' design, the lower two bear 'acanthus-moulding'.

24xxvii–xxviii: A large, artichoke-shaped knop, obviously from a large tureen lid. A comparative example is shown from the 1807 Whitbread catalogue (24xxviii). See also the knop of the sugar bowl illustrated in colour plate 23.

Fig.24xxiii

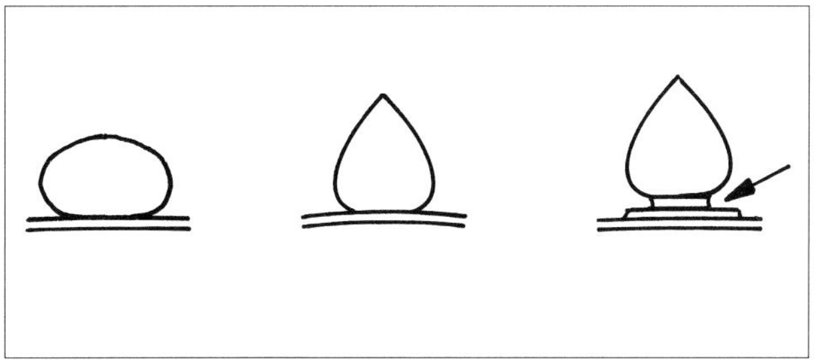

Fig.24xxiv

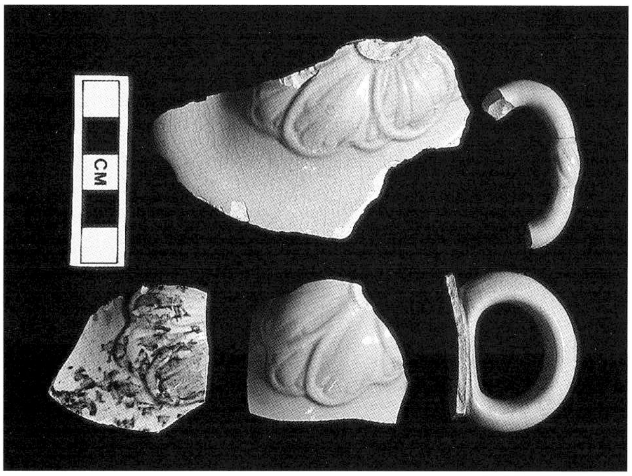

Fig.24xxv

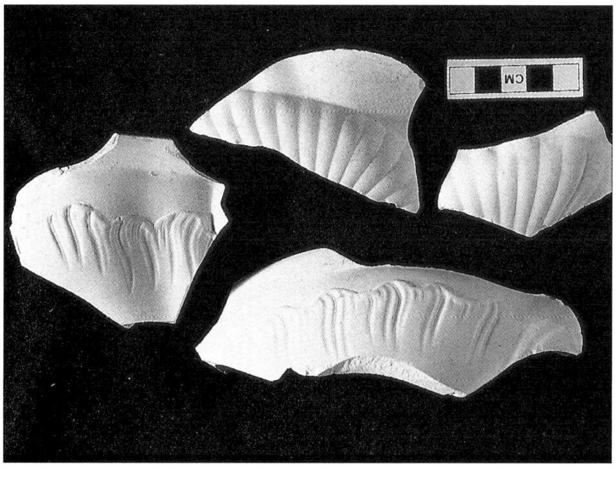

Fig.24xxvi

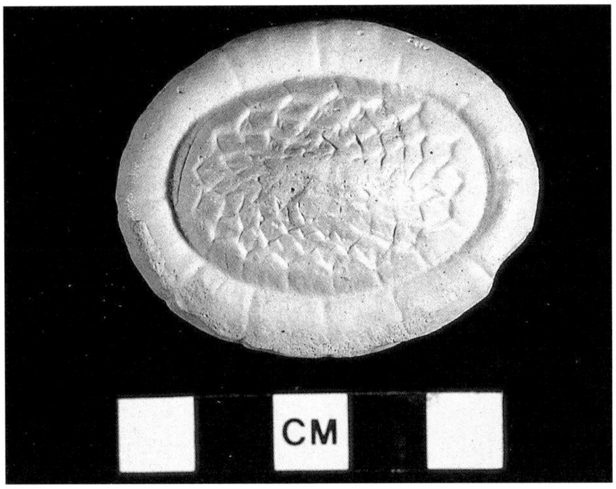

Fig.24xxvii

Fig.25i

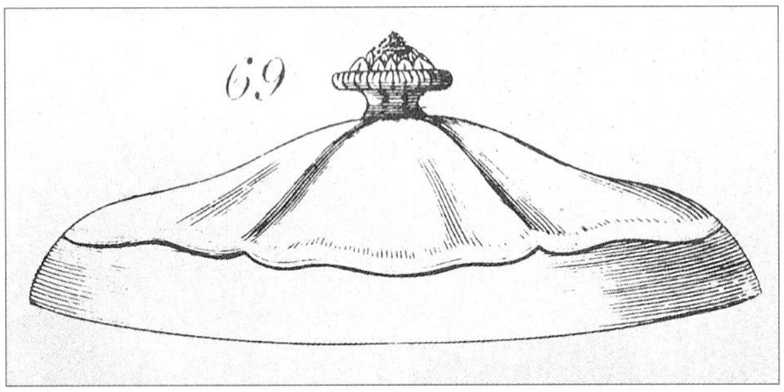

Fig.24xxviii

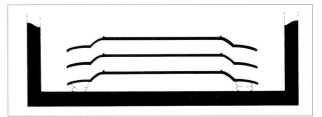

Fig.25ii

25. KILN FURNITURE AND RELATED OBJECTS
(Figs. 25i–25xii)
Discarded kiln furniture, principally consisting of large, broken saggar fragments, constituted by far the most abundant group of finds during the excavation, (more than 80 per cent by weight). Only a small, representative sample of each of the individual forms was retained for the collection.

The kiln furniture encountered appears standard, although the range is small when compared to extensive excavations in England. A thorough published description of kiln furniture is provided by Barker in his account of excavations on the William Greatbatch (creamware) site in Staffordshire, from which text several of the accompanying illustrations are reproduced (25i–25iii). See bibliography.

The standard manufacture of creamware and pearlware demands two firings. The first ('biscuit') firing produces an unglazed, white biscuit-ware body, following which the object is often decorated, dipped in glaze and subjected to a second ('glost') firing. Different types of 'kiln furniture' were employed by the potters for each of these two firings.

Creamware objects were generally placed in large, cylindrical containers called 'saggars' for both firings, (25i), although the stacking arrangement of the flatwares was different in each case. During the first firing, when the plates were unglazed and less prone to stick to one another, it was sufficient to separate them

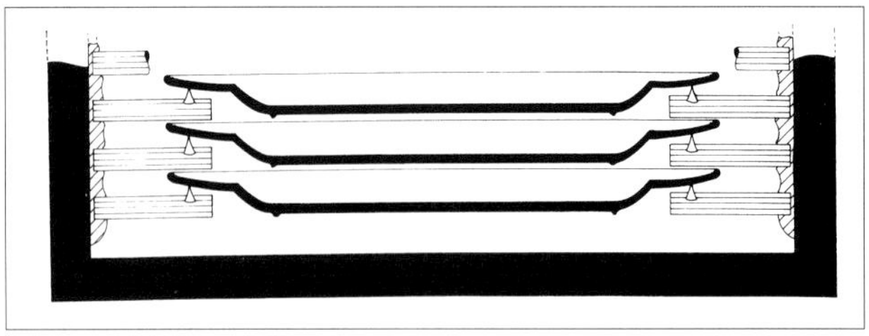

Fig.25iii

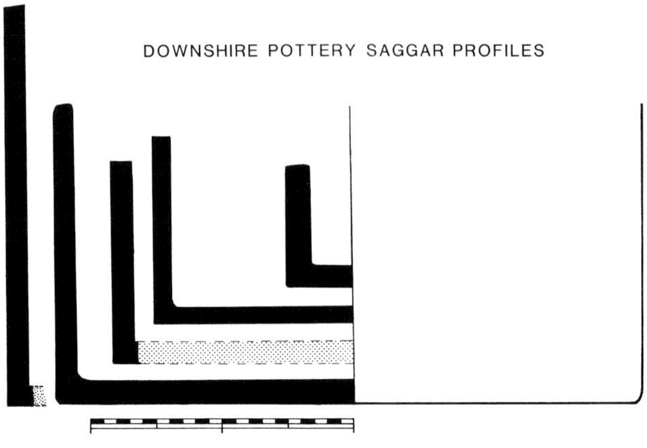

Fig.25iv

with sand (25ii). For the second firing, however, it was particularly important to reduce all areas of contact as much as possible, (to minimise glaze scars) and so the potters produced a large variety of triangular trivets and clay pegs to facilitate this task (25iii).

Other artefacts were encountered during the excavation which, like kiln furniture, were associated with the manufacturing processes; several crucibles, for example, in which raw cobalt may have been refined, and test pieces, for gauging the purity of the cobalt blue colour when fired. Sadly absent were some of the more informative types of potter's artefact that have been found on other sites, such as ceramic block moulds, plaster of Paris moulds and workmen's 'tools' or profiles.

Saggars (Fig. 25iv–v)
There were essentially five different saggar sizes (with minor variations), all were made of light buff, local clay with abundant sand and grit grog. The shapes and sizes of the saggars are illustrated schematically in 25iv.

Height (mm)	Diameter (mm)
1. 90	100
2. 140	300
3. 150	360
4. 225	450
5. 300	c. 520

Crucibles
Unlike saggars, which have a vertical profile, these two small vessels are flared. The inner edge is coated with a highly vitrified off-white glaze and a volatalised cobalt blue ring, which suggests that they may have been employed in the manufacture of cobalt blue pigment.

Height (mm)	Rim diameter (mm)
1. > 100	c. 170
2. > 160	c. 180

Semi-vitrified plate waster (Fig. 25vii)
This unusual waster consists of nine biscuit-ware plate rims that have been fused by extreme over-firing, indicating that dinner plates were stacked at least nine deep during the biscuit firing (without any form of spacer other than sand).

Small trivets ('cockspurs') (Fig. 25viii)
Five sizes were found, with triangular point spacings of 20, 24, 25, 30 and 31 mm.

Large trivets ('stilts') (Fig. 25ix)
Recorded in creamware and occasionally pearlware, in a variety of sizes. Some have traces of glaze colour from contact with fired objects.

Horizontal bars, clay strips (Fig. 25x)
Employed in the glost firing of flatwares in the manner shown in 25iii. (None of the horizontal bars found on the Downshire Pottery site exhibited added points or spurs.)

Glaze-colour test pieces (Fig. 25xi)
Small fragments of cobalt blue painted pearlware, placed in the kiln by the potters to test the fired colour. Some are numbered.

Pencil-written note (Fig. 25xii)
This small biscuit-ware fragment was used as a notepad to record pottery details. Although not entirely legible, it does contain the remark '2 Printed...'. A strange remark, considering that no sign of any printed wares were observed during the excavation.

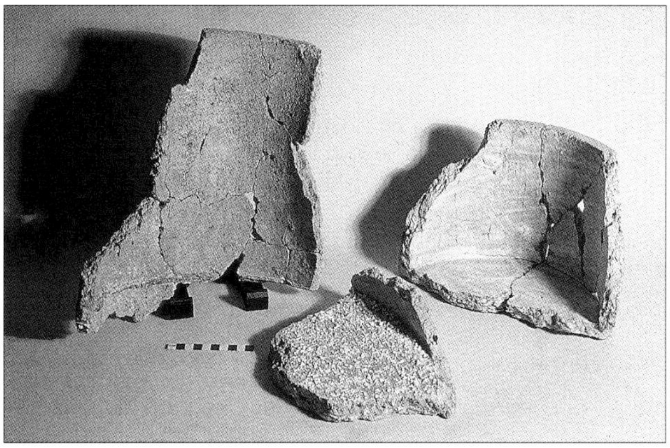

Fig.25v

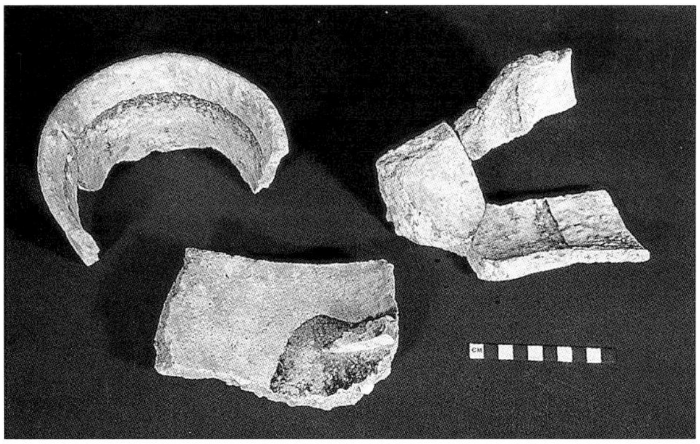

Fig.25vi

Fig.25vii

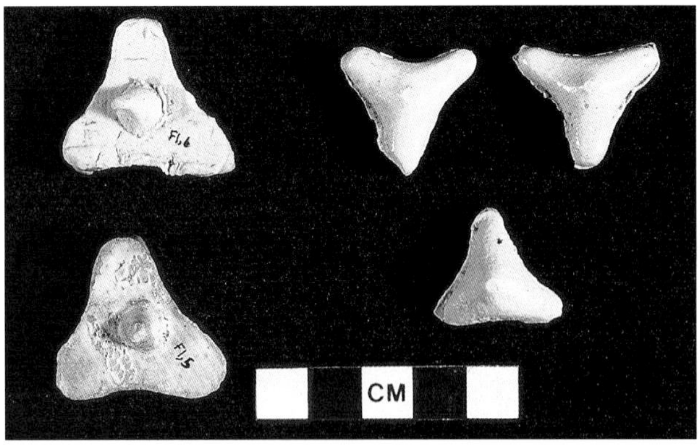

Fig.25viii

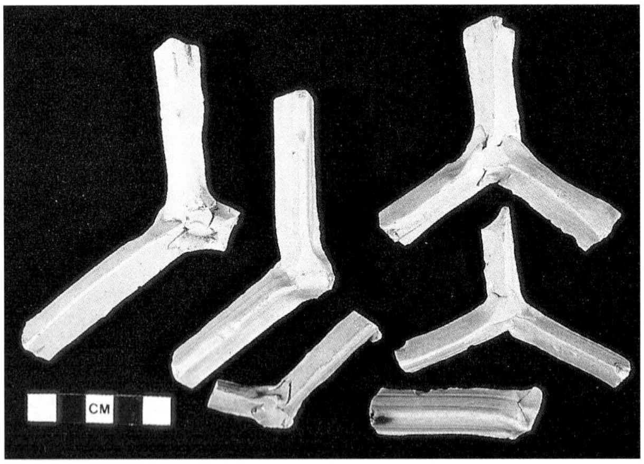

Fig.25ix

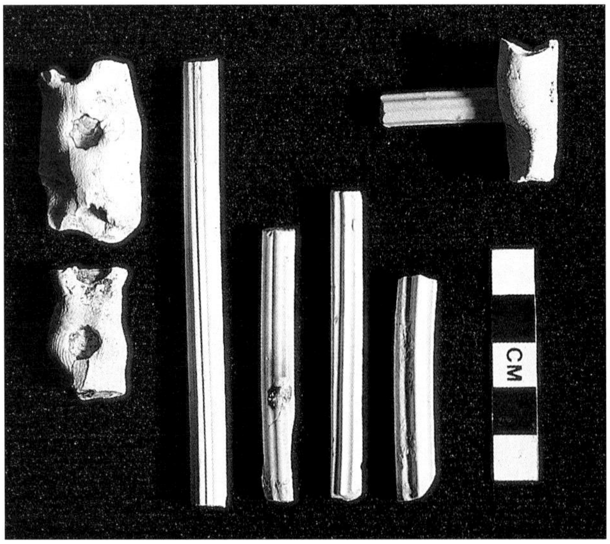

Fig.25x

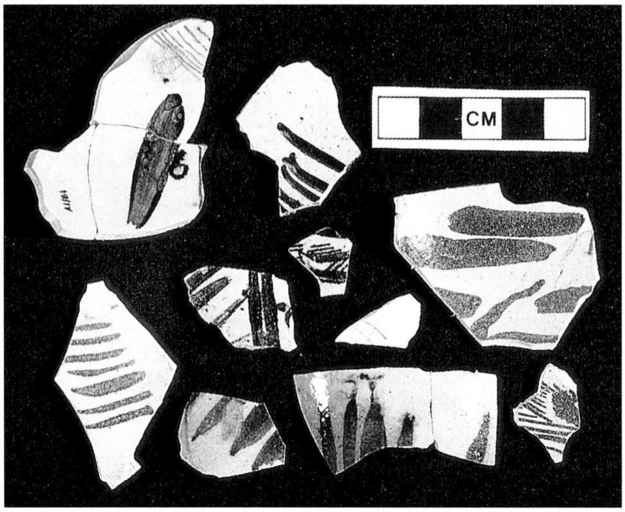

Fig.25xi

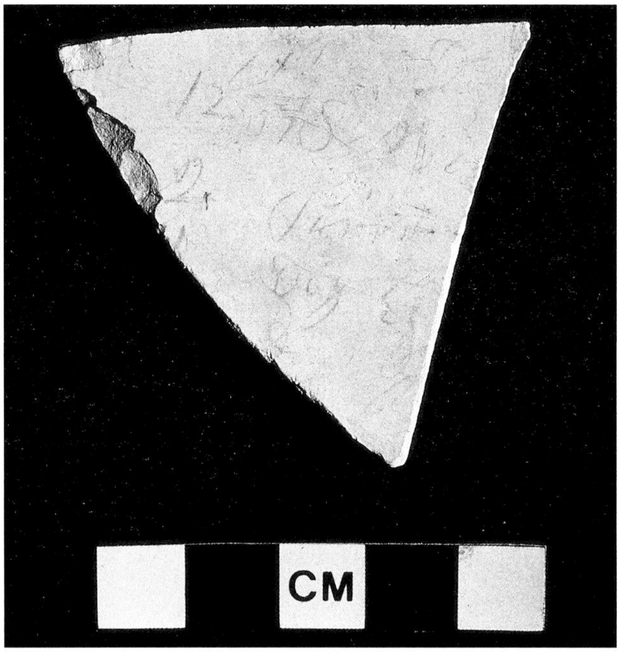

Fig.25xii

SOURCES OF ILLUSTRATIONS

The illustrations in this book are reproduced by kind permission of the following individuals and organisations:

Illustration Source	Figures
Jonathan Rickard	Colour plate 23
Linenhall Library, Belfast	1, 7, 22
Manchester City Art Gallery	4
National Trust, Quarry Bank Mill	59
Council of the Royal Irish Academy	13, JM1, 12ii, 13vi
George Stacpoole, Adare	Colour plate 18
Bonham's, London	Colour plate 19
Sotheby's, London	30
Whitbread catalogue (courtesy David Drakard)	3iv, 6ii, 9ii, 13viii, 14i, 15iii, 18iii, 18iv
Jonathan Horne and David Barker	25i–25iii
Trustees of the National Museums and Galleries of Northern Ireland (Ulster Museum)	6, 8, 10, 19, 20, 21, 25, 4ii, JMii, 11ii, 14vii, colour plates 13–17, 20–23

All other photographs by the author, with kind assistance of the Archaeology Department, Queen's University Belfast and the Ulster Museum

Bibliography

Archer (1979) Michael Archer, *Irish Pottery & Porcelain.* The Irish Heritage Series: 27, Eason & Sons Ltd, Dublin, (1979).

Barker David Barker, *William Greatbatch a Staffordshire Potter,* Jonathan Horne Publications, London, (1991).

Dunlevy (1984) Mairead Dunlevy, 'Irish Fine-Ceramic Potteries, 1769–96', *Post-Mediaeval Archaeology,* Vol. 18, (1984), pp 251–61.

Dunlevy (1988) Mairead Dunlevy, *Ceramics in Ireland,* National Museum of Ireland, (1988).

Francis (1992) Peter Francis, 'The Early Fine-Ceramic Potteries of Belfast & the Carrickfergus Clay Trade', unpublished MA thesis, Archaeology Department, Queen's University Belfast, (1992).

Francis (1995) Peter Francis, 'Irish Creamware, the Downshire Pottery in Belfast', *English Ceramic Circle Transactions,* Vol 15, Pt 3, (1995), pp 400–25.

Francis (1997) Peter Francis, 'Recent Discoveries in Irish Ceramics', *Irish Arts Review Yearbook,* Vol 13, (1997), pp 88–101.

Francis (2000) Peter Francis, *Irish Delftware:* an Illustrated History, Jonathan Horne Publications, London, (2000).

Towner (1963) Donald Towner, *The Leeds Pottery,* London, (1963).

Towner (1978) Donald Towner, *Creamware,* Faber, London, (1978).

Walton (1976) Peter Walton, *Creamware and other English Pottery at Temple Newsam House, Leeds,* Manningham Press, Bradford and London, (1976).

Westrop (1913) MS Dudley Westropp, 'Notes on the Pottery Manufacture in Ireland', *Proceedings of the Royal Irish Academy,* Vol XXXII, Section C, No 1, Dublin, (1913).

Westropp (1935) MS Dudley Westropp, *General Guide to the Art Collections: Pottery and Porcelain,* National Museum of Ireland, Dublin, (1935).

English Creamware Pattern Books

The Castleford Pottery Pattern Book, 1796, facsimile edition, EP Publishing Ltd (1973).

The Don Pottery Pattern Book, 1807, facsimile edition, Doncaster Metropolitan Council, (1983).

Leeds Pottery, 1783 and 1794. Reprinted in full in Towner (1963).

St Anthony's Pottery, Newcastle upon Tyne, (c 1815), facsimile edition, Northern Ceramic Society and Tyne & Wear Museums, (1993).

Wedgwood, 1774, reprinted in Wolf Mankowitz, *Wedgwood,* Spring Books, London (1996), pl 1–13.

The Whitehead Catalogue, 1798, facsimile edition, David B Drakard, (n d, c 1973).